D1232979

METROPOLITICS:
THE NASHVILLE CONSOLIDATION

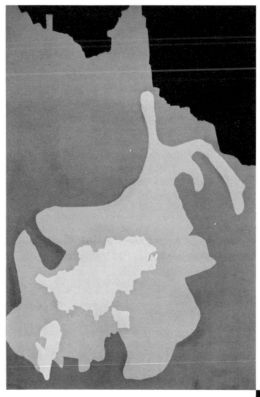

by DAVID A. BOOTH

Institute for Community Development and Services Michigan State University
1963

JS
451
T39
.N33
1963

352.0768551
B725m

Copyright © 1963
By the Board of Trustees
Michigan State University
East Lansing, Michigan
Price: $2.00

Library of Congress Catalog Card Number:
63-62529

LIBRARY
FLORIDA STATE UNIVERSITY
TALLAHASSEE, FLORIDA.

iv

CONTENTS

TABLES

vii

MAPS

INTRODUCTION

A CASE study can do more than to describe a series of events in a particular community, as has been demonstrated by several local government studies, such as those of Dahl in New Haven and Sayre and Kaufman in New York. It is obvious that if they could do no more, they could contribute little to the development of a science of politics. David Booth's study of Nashville and Davidson County does much more than merely to describe the actors and the action related to campaigns for a metropolitan form of government. It also:

(1) Offers a comparative study in which is told two stories having the same locale; one a story of frustration, the other of success.

(2) Adds to the scarce supply of information regarding attitudes toward metropolitan government, and the attitudinal environment within which advocates of change operate.

(3) Provides some how-to-do-it hints for those working for change in other metropolitan areas.

(4) Raises a number of questions of the sort that are likely to be useful in the development of a general theory of metropolitan structural change and of metropolitan decision-making generally.

As to the first of these points, the story speaks for itself. The fact that an analysis of the second (successful) campaign is not as fully covered as the first is not the fault of the author. Time considerations and distance from the scene are important limitations. It seems, in light of the short time between adoption and the effectuation of the plan, desirable to publish this report without further delay.

The information on citizen attitudes, categorized by class and education, is significant in itself but is especially valuable for theory building because it generally conforms to the findings in Dayton and St. Louis. It gives some indications of the importance of group values to campaigns

1

for metropolitan reorganization. Perceptions of access to governmental decision-makers and the representativeness of officeholders is an important aspect of any political environment — a fact often seemingly forgotten by reformers. Its relevance to political campaigns is here sharply called to the attention of community activists.

The how-to-do-it aspects of this study must be discovered by the proverbial reading between the lines. The author did not seek to discover any success formulas, magical or otherwise. Yet, the activist can find much here that is relevant to his particular trade. The empirical data collected after the first (unsuccessful) attempt at consolidation, for example, indicate that members of groups exposed to propaganda voted significantly more in favor of the integration plan than did others. On the first attempt, the proponents depended largely on the mediums of mass communication and reached relatively few persons (especially those below the upper-middle-class levels) in the friendly environment of their own reference and associational groups. But on the second try, the strategists switched to the approach of contacting people directly and making a "pitch" for the plan in the meeting rooms of various groups and under the sponsorship of persons trusted by the voter being wooed. This is what the empirical data indicated was the better part of wisdom — and the approach worked (or at least the proponents won, and there is a widespread opinion that the change in strategy was a significant factor.)

Similarly, we find that on the first try the activists made little progress seeking to gain support through use of rational arguments based on the assumed logic of their position. Prior to the second try, however, Nashville had launched an aggressive annexation campaign which had caused considerable uneasiness to many a suburbanite. When it came time for a second vote, he seems to have supported the Metro plan as a matter of "negative" voting — as a less undesirable alternative than that of being absorbed into the city of

2

Nashville by unilateral annexation. The second type of appeal, in other words, was that of a sort that would be meaningful to any professional politician; the first type was one that would not be. The how-to-do-it lesson should be obvious: metropolitics is still politics; its successful techniques are likely to be those that work in other aspects of American politics; the professional politician is likely to be a better tactician than the dedicated and earnest do-gooder.

As to the questions that are raised, they are of more than ordinary interest to social scientists. They are not the usual lame suggestions for "further research" with which the typical empirical study concludes today. These questions are highly relevant to the development of a theory of metropolitan decision-making. Here are only a few of them:

What proportion of the successful campaign in Nashville can be attributed to the annexation laws of Tennessee? These laws are free and easy when compared with those of neighboring Kentucky, where the legal alternative, incorporation along the outer fringe, is simple. Louisville is, as a result, surrounded by over 50 incorporated suburbs. Could the Nashville approach ever be successful in Louisville? If the answer is "no," what are the implications, if any, of this difference in legal environment? What has been the trend in changes in incorporation and annexation laws in the various states? How do the changes correlate with rates of incorporation and annexation? In general, what part of the occasional successes of metropolitan integration plans can be explained by legal environment? This question was once one of central concern in metropolitan-area writings. It was later scorned by process-oriented political scientists, but now may be a fruitful area of further inquiry through use of modern statistical techniques and of high-speed data-processing equipment. Perhaps we will one day be able to anticipate changes in governmental structure of metropolitan areas on the basis of knowledge flowing from research such as this.

Among the many other questions raised in this study are some related to strategies for metropolitan change. What are optimum strategies for victory in a metropolitan integration proposal? I do not conclude that the proponents *should* win, only that this study seems to point to a number of lessons they might learn if they wish to do so. In the past, the opponents of change have held most of the high cards, including the advantage of having the superior political strategists — the professional politicians — on their side. Reformers, being educated persons who view their approach as highly rational, have strongly tended to accept the eighteenth-century rational man as a model for the metropolitan voter. The "pro" — who knows better than to do so — thus reached more people and reached them in a telling fashion. In Nashville, strategies in the two campaigns were very different. The second time, a serious effort was made to reach the voter in his own environment — hundreds of meetings were held — and by using arguments made meaningful through appeals to his anxieties and aspirations, the technique was to use symbols and play upon emotions, as the practicing politician long ago learned to do. No one has yet written a monograph dealing with such questions as: What are the emotional and symbolic assets available to the advocate of metropolitan reorganization? How can they be brought effectively into use in a campaign? How does one effectively counter negative symbols with positive symbols? What anxieties of the potential "no" voter can be exploited so as to produce a switch to "yes"? (In Nashville, it was the fear of annexation to the central city.) What aspirations of citizens can be appealed to effectively? That is, how can people be led to believe that there is a causal relationship between an integrated governmental structure and their *personal* hopes for the future? Some reformers will be reluctant to admit that the ordinary tool kit of the practicing

4

politician should be used to repair metropolitan governmental machinery. The story of Nashville hints that perhaps they would be wise to cease being squeamish.

I commend to you the story that follows. Whatever your beliefs about metropolitan-area government, wherever your interests in the subject may lie, there is likely to be something here for you.

CHARLES R. ADRIAN

AUTHOR'S PREFACE

THE TREND towards megalopolis continues. Over 70 per cent of the American people now live in urban places, and demographers estimate that up to 90 million more persons may do so in the next 20 years. The intricacies and interdependencies of urban living have assumed proportions that attract the attention of many groups. Civil Defense experts seek ways to reduce vulnerability from thermonuclear attack. Scholars and planners weigh and measure various procedures, policies, and plans that have been devised to meet the endless needs and problems occasioned by unplanned and unchecked population growth. Politicians, administrators and voters tussle with alternatives which often turn out to be mere palliatives. Notwithstanding their efforts, few areas are at present governed under forms which can withstand the stresses endemic to rapid urbanization and meet the changing needs of a growing population.

One approach that has so far found more favor with planners and ideal-model builders than with voters and politicians is city-county consolidation. This entails the merging of the functions of a city and an adjoining or surrounding county into a new unit of metropolitan government. The difficulties which lie in the path of consolidation are such that they have severely limited the number of attempts made during the last two decades. Even when these difficulties are surmounted, metropolitan plans have usually been rejected by the voters when submitted for adoption.

Empirical investigations into such decisions are few in number, and a basic question, still largely unanswered, is why the solutions devised have generally proved to be politically unacceptable to the electorate. The question is intrinsically important, but is made more so by the several consolidation plans that are now in the planning stages in several communities throughout the land.

6

The question has no single answer, as many obstacles lie in the path of governmental reorganization. Metro plans now generally face the passage of a constitutional amendment or an enabling act; they must run the gauntlet of officeholders who enjoy the status and rewards that public office brings them, but which they might lose in the event of governmental reorganization. Such plans may face the opposition of certain interest groups which fear the dilution of their political influence. They must win the support of an apathetic public concerned with low taxes, having a voice in government and their own suburban life-styles rather than with accountability, efficiency, or economy in their local government. Finally, they must compete for public favor, not only against the status quo, but against other less dramatic solutions to community problems, such as annexation. Thus, it is not surprising that the political process involves the decisions of many groups and individuals. It is probably molded by hidden forces which remain undetected during an investigation.

Not all metro plans are defeated. An unusual departure from the pattern of defeat recently occurred in Tennessee, when, on June 28, 1962, the voters of the city of Nashville and of Davidson County together voted to merge their respective units of local government into a new metropolitan unit. An earlier attempt, made in 1958, had failed.

This monograph deals with these two attempts. It focuses first upon the 1958 attempt and upon three different groups of decision-makers who contributed, either directly or indirectly, to the 1958 defeat. This is primarily a study in community decision-making in three different arenas. The events leading up to the second vote and its successful outcome are discussed in a final chapter.

This study in metropolitics combines and synthesizes the results of three field investigations conducted in the Nashville area during the last four years and of other more recent fact-finding visits to the community. Some friends and former colleagues from Vanderbilt University participated in some of them. Chapter Two is in joint authorship with Daniel R. Grant and is based on the results of research undertaken with him. Chapter Three is based on data obtained in a joint research project undertaken with J. Leiper Freeman and Jeanne Clare Ridley. It is written in collaboration with Paul Alexander, who used part of the data for his M.A. thesis. Much of the field work was accomplished by political science and sociology students of Vanderbilt University. The original cost of these studies was borne by the Falk Foundation, through its grant to the Political Science Department, Vanderbilt University. More recent expenses connected with this research were borne by the Institute for Community Development, Michigan State University.

It is customary to thank all those who have helped to make this study possible, and I do so now. I wish to thank the editors of the *Municipal South* for giving me permission to use material previously published in June, 1962. I especially wish to thank Robert A. Horton of the Nashville-Davidson County Planning Commission Staff, who has read and criticized several chapters and given me much friendly help, advice and encouragement. Also, I wish to acknowledge my gratitude to the editor, Isabelle Brymer, and to Robert Becker and Alan Arcuri, who assisted me in the preparation of the manuscript. Finally, I wish to thank Charles R. Adrian, Director of the Institute for Community Development, who made it possible for me to complete this study and who graciously consented to prepare an introduction.

DAVID A. BOOTH
East Lansing, Michigan
November, 1962

METROPOLITICS:

THE NASHVILLE CONSOLIDATION

Chapter One

THE SETTING, THE PROBLEMS AND THE CONSOLIDATION PROPOSAL

The Setting

The "Volunteer State" of Tennessee has been called a narrow ribbon of real estate stretching from North Carolina to the banks of the lazy Mississippi. The great seal of the state features two words, "Agriculture" and "Commerce", emphasizing the dominance of farming in the state's economy. Between the two rather different geographical extremes lies Middle Tennessee, a fertile bowl known locally as the "dimple of the Universe." It is dominated by the state's capital, Nashville, and densely populated Davidson County which covers an area of 533 square miles. The county includes a handful of small suburban cities scattered around Nashville. Some are dormitory suburbs, closely linked to the core city; others are more independent, and their citizens apparently take some pride in their independence from the "big city folk."

Radio announcers may be heard to claim that Nashville is the "leading city of the central South." Perhaps it is too bold a claim, even though the city has some important assets. The city, founded in 1784, is situated in the middle of the county on a bend in the Cumberland River. It is a capital city with a rich historical past, having been the home of Andrew Jackson, the nation's President from 1828 to 1836. More recently, it has become an educational and cultural center. It is the home of several institutions of higher learning, including Fisk University, Tennessee A and I, Vanderbilt University and George Peabody College. A full-scale replica of the Parthenon, set in a large public park, gives the city an additional claim to the title "the Athens of the South."

11

Nashville is well served by highways, railroads and airlines; the latter use a recently completed multimillion dollar airport. The city has well-established industries in chemicals, metal products, leather, shoes and glass. It is an important center of white collar occupations in printing, publishing, insurance and banking. Finally, it is the nation's capital for the recording and manufacture of popular and "mountain" music records.[1]

In other respects, the claim to leadership does not seem unreasonable. Nashville was one of the first Southern cities to introduce a gradual program of school integration in the wake of the Supreme Court decisions. Though faced with bombings and agitators, the city nevertheless has steadily progressed in the problem of granting Negroes equality before the law.

Middle Tennessee is dominated by the Democratic party, but the party struggle plays a very limited part in local government.[2] On the local level, Davidson County is governed by a quarterly county court, which is essentially a rural type of local government.[3] Executive authority is vested in a popularly elected county judge, serving an eight-year term. Nashville is governed by a city council and by a popularly elected mayor. It has the strong-mayor type of government.

The Problems of the County and City

Many of the problems common to large cities are found in Nashville and its surrounding area. Some are caused by the topography of the land. Hills surround the city, and this has meant that smoke and smog are slow to clear on cold damp winter mornings; thus, the city faces a very serious smoke abatement problem. The county's subsoil is thin and mostly underlaid with limestone, making it unsuitable for septic tanks. The river has facilitated industrial growth but has engendered certain disadvantages. Some of its low-lying plains are liable to floods, making these

12

areas unsuitable for residential or industrial development. The river also serves to divide the city, and class distinctions have developed along spatial lines, demarcated by the river.

Other problems have been caused by increases and shifts in population. Rapid population growth on the fringes of other large cities have led to real and urgent problems.[4] Such areas suddenly find themselves in need of a water supply, sewage disposal, and storm drainage. The building and staffing of schools become urgent necessities, as do the construction and maintenance of arterial highways which can handle the growing armies of daily commuters to the core city.[5]

Within the last two decades the population of Davidson County increased by 25 per cent. The population of the central city, however, remained constant between 1940 and 1950, and actually declined since 1950. The principal changes in population since 1950 are presented in Table 1,

TABLE 1

Davidson County and Nashville, Tennessee Population Data, 1950 - 1960

	Davidson County		Nashville	
	1950	1960	1950	1960
Total population	321,758	399,743	174,307	170,874[a]
Percentage nonwhite	20.0	19.2	31.4	37.9
Households	88,705	114,635	49,748	50,990

[a] The 1960 figure includes 4,587 persons added to the central city by the 1958 annexation of 6.91 square miles of industrial and commercial land.

Source: U. S. Bureau of the Census.

which indicates that in 1960, the population of the county was approximately 400,000 persons and less than half of them lived in the core city.

The problems caused by the shifts in population have been in the making for many years. At the root of them all is the fact that the central city annexation program failed to keep pace with pop-

13

ulation growth, and that by the early 1950's, the city limits did not even closely correspond to the urbanized area, as shown on Map 1. The problems of population growth have been compounded by the fact that the county government

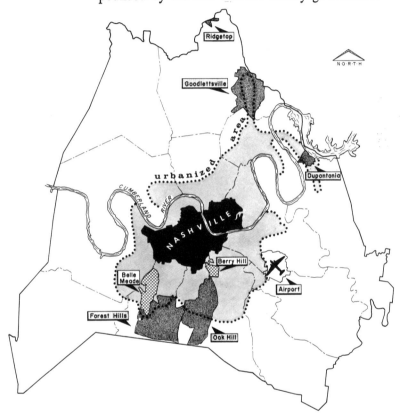

MAP 1.—Incorporated Cities and Urbanized Area of Davidson County, Tennessee.

was not structured so that it could easily or readily provide for the needs of 125,000 persons living under conditions of population density requiring urban services.[6]

Consequently, a large part of the area outside Nashville was not served by urban facilities. Services such as police and fire protection, and

14

garbage collection were provided on a private subscription basis, and were makeshift, inefficient and inadequate. There was no sanitary sewer system; no coordination of the various systems of fire protection outside Nashville; inadequate police protection; and an almost complete absence of street lights and sidewalks in the suburbs. An inadequate water supply forced some areas to buy water from the core city and others to rely on monopolistic private water companies. This shortage of water increased the danger of fire, resulting in higher insurance rates.

No local government was able to cope with these problems, which frequently cross-cut boundary lines and which professionals believe are best solved by area-wide solutions. Consequently, the problems of water supply, the control and prevention of crime, juvenile delinquency, traffic flow, fire protection and immunization programs were not receiving proper attention. The two school systems existing side by side produced duplication and waste, with vacant city classrooms and overcrowded county schools.

Some duplication had gradually been eliminated in the 1950's such as in public health, welfare and the two Planning Commissions sharing a single professional staff. In most matters, however, the county and city continued to maintain two separate bureaucracies with their endemic political encrustations. Many observers in the area believed that the existence of separate city and county governments was wasteful and tended to needlessly divide the community along artificial lines.

Such divisions were thought to dissipate popular control and to weaken the democratic process. The divided structure of local government did not permit the public to determine who had responsibility and authority to enforce policies. The lack of over-all jurisdiction meant that suburbanites had to pay taxes and fees to several different legal entities for the various

15

services rendered, making it difficult to exercise proper supervision over them.

Nashville also had its problems, typical of those faced by other large cities.[8] It was confronted with the daily influx of a vast army of suburbanites who earned their living in the city, but lived outside the city's tax jurisdiction. Thus, the core city had to provide all sorts of free services to this daylight invasion, including city parks, libraries, costly avenues of transportation, parking facilities, and law and traffic enforcement and regulation. The city also had a financial problem. Many of the business interests in the city were charitable or religious enterprises, and were beyond the city's taxing power. The declining population meant a declining tax base. Also, the tax base was being eroded by the large percentage of low-income Negroes living in the city (see Table 1) who generally contributed little to property tax revenue. The city had not been politically reapportioned for over 30 years, leading to inequities in political representation. Finally, like other cities throughout the country, Nashville received less than its per capita share of various county and state taxes.

The Origin of Metro

The original impetus of the metropolitan government idea stemmed from studies undertaken by the Community Services Commission for Davidson County and the city of Nashville. Its report, entitled *A Future for Nashville,* issued on June 1, 1952, alleged that there was needless duplication in city and county functions. The report recommended annexation of most of the surrounding urbanized area by the core city since consolidation of the two legal entities seemed impracticable because of the constitutional bar on establishing two tax rates.

In 1953, a constitutional convention submitted several amendments to the people of Tennessee. One amendment provided for the consolidation

16

of any or all functions of a city and county by means of concurrent majorities inside and outside the central city. Furthermore, it seemed to provide clearance for separate tax rates which had previously been barred. In 1955, the Davidson County and Nashville Planning Commissions initiated studies. The main problem facing them was the lack of a sewerage system in the county, but the other problems outlined above were believed to be interrelated. As a result, it was concluded that a unified approach to all the metropolitan problems relating to public services and utilities was the most feasible solution.

By the fall of 1955, it was clear that a question of governmental organization was involved, and a consultant in metropolitan government was brought into the planning. Studies were undertaken in order to solve the problem of metropolitan disintegration. After considering the merits of alternative solutions, and in view of the governmental structure, it was decided that the best solution would be to bring about the consolidation of the city and county into one unit of government. This was the basic recommendation of a report issued by both Planning Commissions in October 1956.[9]

A general act authorizing the creation of a Metropolitan Government Charter Commission was sponsored by members of the Davidson County Legislative Delegation and was adopted by the State Legislature in 1957.[10] Both the city and county local government bodies gave their tentative consent to the proposal by creating a Metropolitan Charter Commission and making the necessary funds available. Next, the mayor and the county judge appointed a group of distinguished civic leaders to serve as the Charter Commission, including several well-known attorneys and a Negro councilman. After a long series of meetings, a Charter was drawn up and its main provisions made known in February,

17

1958. It was filed a month later, on March 28, and eventually published and distributed throughout the community.

The 1958 Reform Proposal

The purpose of the proposal was to consolidate the functions of the city and the county into a single "Metropolitan Government of Nashville and Davidson County." Legislative authority was to be vested in a representative metropolitan council of 21 members, replacing the city council and the county quarterly court. The city mayor and the county judge would have been replaced by a popularly elected chief executive entitled metropolitan mayor.

The new metropolitan government would have exercised its jurisdiction through two service districts. A *general services district* would have consisted of the whole area, while the *urban services district* would consist of that part of the area to be furnished urban services. In addition, the Charter provided for two tax rates to coincide with the service districts; and it stipulated that the urban type services must be provided within one year after the urban tax rate became due.

While the plan did not envisage complete unification of all city and county functions, a considerable amount of unification would have been achieved. The duplication in the administration of schools, hospitals, streets and roads, tax assessment and in many other functions of local government would have been eliminated.

The cluster of small suburban cities surrounding Nashville (see Map 1) would have become part of the new government, including the general services district. On the other hand, such cities were intended to retain their incorporated status until a majority of the population decided otherwise. The citizens of such cities were able to vote in the referendum without affecting the status of their own place of residence.

18

The brunt of the campaign in support of Metro was borne by the two Nashville newspapers, *The Tennessean* (morning and Sunday) and *The Banner* (afternoon daily). Though they use the same publishing facilities and are housed in the same building, the two papers keep up an intense rivalry. They are normally opposed on almost every issue, and their common support of the proposal was a departure from their usual practice.

Both newspapers devoted a great deal of space to the campaign, and extensive use was made of feature stories, cartoons, editorials and guest articles by well-known local personages who authored a series of articles entitled "I Like Metro Because . . . ." Both newspapers assigned at least one reporter on a full-time basis to the proposal. In retrospect, it is hard to see how either of the papers could have done more to bring about the adoption of the plan.

The Nashville Chamber of Commerce played an important, if unobtrusive, role in the campaign.[11] It maintained an active interest in the activities of the Planning Commission and worked to gain the enabling legislation for the referendum. It nominated the members, organized the offices, and set the goals of the Citizen's Committee which formally guided the campaign, and anonymously paid for a four-page newspaper advertisement presenting the plan for Metro to the citizens of the community.[12] The advertisement pointed out that the absence of a sanitary sewer system outside the city limits was a handicap to the industrial development of the community, and asserted that consolidated government would remedy that specific problem, and that the community would also derive other economic benefits from Metropolitan Government. The Board of Governors of the Chamber of Commerce unanimously approved the Charter in its final form.

The Citizen's Committee for Metropolitan Government bore the responsibility of presenting Metro to the public in the final months before the referendum. Since it had only a limited budget, its activities were severely hampered.[13] The Committee financed the printing of 10,000 copies of the Charter, was responsible for an essay contest in the schools, and provided a panel of available speakers who spoke to a limited number of groups, both in the city and in the county, discussing the provisions of the Charter and urging its adoption by the public.

Other efforts to persuade the public included sporadic presentations of Metro on radio and television and the distribution, through department stores, of 10,000 copies of the Charter and 50,000 copies of a short pamphlet, "You and Metropolitan Government." No attempt was made to organize a "grass roots" organization in support of the proposal; in retrospect, this seems to have been a fundamental oversight on the part of the Committee.

The Charter was endorsed by the city mayor and the county judge, the two leading politicians of Davidson County. Though it is doubtful if either maximized the use of their political organizations, both advocated the adoption of the plan.[14] In addition, the proposal was given considerable backing by other community leaders, by several civic groups, and by reform-oriented groups, such as the League of Women Voters.

The opposition to the consolidation plan was much more clandestine, remaining largely silent and hidden until about a week before the vote, when it unleashed a bitter whirl-wind attack. The plan was attacked on many grounds, and was even alleged to be inspired by the communist plot to take over the world. Spot announcements on the radio were used to urge defeat of the proposal, and one well-known rural politician made a television address attacking the proposal. Leaflets were given out on streets and on buses and also through the county school teachers to their pupils.

Apparently most of the opposition came from some members of the Quarterly County Court, from county school teachers' organizations and from private suburban fire and police companies which would have been largely driven out of business with the adoption of the plan. The proposal was also opposed by many suburban merchants and businessmen, who apparently feared renewed competition from the central business district, in the event of consolidation.[15]

The Voting and the Outcome

The Tennessee Constitutional Amendment and the General Enabling Act stipulate that city-county consolidation can be effected only by favorable votes in both areas to be consolidated. As has often been the case elsewhere,[16] the defeat of Metro in the Nashville area was caused by an adverse vote outside the central city. In a light turnout, the city voted in favor, but the surrounding county, in a heavier turnout, defeated the proposal.[17] A simple breakdown of the voting is presented in Table 2, showing that the opposition to Metro was heaviest outside the city of Nashville and that it became proportionately more intense as the distance increased from the central city.

The defeat was not surprising and, in many ways, was typical of the failures of other consolidation plans which have occurred during the last

TABLE 2

Popular Vote For and Against Metro in Davidson County Referendum, June 17, 1958

	For	Against	Per Cent For
Urban (City of Nashville)	7,797	4,808	61.9
Contiguous Suburban	11,130	10,065	52.5
Noncontiguous Suburban	2,105	5,998	26.0
Rural	555	3,727	14.9

Source: *National Municipal Review*, XLVII (September, 1958), 399.

decade.[18] The proponents certainly failed to anticipate the intensity of the opposition, and the whole consolidation proposal lacked a crucial issue to arouse the interest of the citizenry. Some of the other reasons which led to defeat are discussed in the next three chapters, which deal in turn with the city and county local government legislators, the suburbanites who defeated the proposal, and the top leadership group of the community.

FOOTNOTES TO CHAPTER ONE

[1] A useful reference book is *The Tennessee Blue Book: Reference Edition,* Annual (Nashville: Office of the Secretary of State).

[2] See V. O. Key, Jr., *Southern Politics in State and Nation* (New York: Alfred Knopf, Inc., 1949), ch. 4. Also an unusual series of articles by David Halberstam in *The Reporter,* XIX (September 4, 1958), 24-26; XXII (March 31, 1960), 17-19; XXIII (September 1, 1960), 24-30; XXIV (January 19, 1961), 40-41.

[3] The first Davidson County Court met on October 6, 1783. Two of the first acts of the court were orders to clear a road from Nashborough (now Nashville) to Manker's Station; and authorization for a ferry to cross the river. See Cartter Patten, *A Tennessee Chronicle* (Nashville, 1953), 73. It is interesting to note that 180 years later, one of the main problems is still roads and bridges.

[4] William N. Leonard, "Economic Aspects of Suburbanization," *The Suburban Community,* ed. William M. Dobriner (New York: G. P. Putnam and Sons, 1958), 181-194.

[5] Charles R. Adrian, *Governing Urban America,* 2nd ed. (New York: McGraw-Hill Book Co., 1961), chs. 1, 2 & 11.

[6] The problems of the area were summarized by Daniel R. Grant in "Urban and Suburban Nashville: A Case Study in Metropolitanism," *Journal of Politics,* XVII (February, 1955), 82-89.

[7] The point is developed by Robert C. Wood, *Suburbia, Its People and Their Politics* (Boston: Houghton Mifflin Co., 1959), 254.

[8] See Harry R. Betters (ed.), *City Problems of 1960* (Washington: United States Conference of Mayors, 1960), which contains several provocative essays on urban problems.

22

[9] *Plan of Metropolitan Government for Nashville and Davidson County* (Nashville, October, 1956).

[10] Chapter 120, Public Acts of 1957.

[11] The discussion of the role of the Chamber of Commerce and of the Citizen's Committee is largely drawn from William Paul Alexander, "The Effects of Group Exposure to Campaign Propaganda Upon Voting Behavior in a Nonpartisan Referendum," (Unpublished M. A. Thesis, Vanderbilt University, 1961), 12-16.

[12] The advertisement summarized the problems of the community and the solutions proposed by the Planning Commission. It appeared in *The Nashville Tennessean,* October 30, 1956.

[13] The entire operating fund was approximately $6,000, most of which was used to pay the salary of a full-time executive director, a young attorney who was hired four months before the referendum.

[14] The role of these and other leaders is discussed more extensively in Chapter 4.

[15] Daniel R. Grant and Lee S. Greene, "Surveys, Dust, Action," *National Civic Review,* L (October, 1961), 470.

[16] On December 12, 1961, the voters of Henrico County voted against consolidation with the city of Richmond, Virginia. More recently, on November 6, 1962, the proposal to consolidate Shelby County and Memphis, Tennessee was defeated as it failed to obtain the concurrent majorities prescribed by law.

[17] In Nashville, 22.2 per cent of registered voters went to the polls, while in Davidson County 43.8 per cent voted. The low turnout in the city is partly explained by its large Negro population.

[18] Advisory Commission on Intergovermental Relations, *Factors Affecting Voter Reactions to Governmental Reorganization in Metropolitan Areas* (Washington: U. S. Government Printing Office, 1962), 16-33.

Chapter Two

METRO AND LOCAL GOVERNMENT LEGISLATORS*

One method of studying the politics of a campaign for metropolitan government is to look at the issues and forces involved as seen through the eyes of the elected representatives of the people. While this method admittedly presents only a limited picture of the political process, it can serve to throw some light on the city and county legislators themselves.

Members of the city council and the county court were directly involved in the Nashville-Davidson County consolidation proposal, since it was by their action that the Charter Commission was created and the necessary funds were appropriated. Councilman and magistrates were personally involved in the outcome since the adoption of the plan would have abolished their 22 council positions and the 53 court positions, with only 21 metropolitan council seats created as replacement.[1] Thus, the 1958 Referendum seemed to present an ideal opportunity to observe the apparent conflict of interest between the politicians' interests in the community and their perceptions of their own political future. The purpose of this chapter is to describe the local legislators' views of the Metro issue and to analyze these views in terms of selected variables. The analysis is based on the results of interviews with 18 city councilmen of Nashville and 45 magistrates of Davidson County's Quarterly Court, which were conducted in the period immediately prior to the referendum on June 17, 1958.[2]

In the interview, respondents were asked to indicate their personal view toward the metropolitan government proposal; their interest in it; and their professed familiarity with the Charter.

* This chapter was written jointly with Daniel R. Grant of Vanderbilt University.

They were also asked to predict the outcome of the vote; to explain their prediction; and finally, to identify the groups whom they thought would benefit or lose from the adoption of the Charter.

The relevance of these data rests upon two important assumptions. The first is that the people's elected representatives, in both the city and the county, were sufficiently close to their constituents to be aware of and to understand the forces supporting or opposing a reorganization of governmental structure. Support for this assumption is found in the fact that over 80 per cent of the respondents correctly predicted the outcome of the referendum.

The second assumption is that the views and attitudes of the local legislators toward Metro are generally typical of those of their constituents, and therefore provide some important clues to the public's reactions to the Metro proposal. Corroboration for this assumption is found in the fact that a positive correlation exists between the individual views of most of the local legislators and the way in which their own constituency voted. In 65 per cent of the cases in which respondents expressed their own personal support or opposition to the plan, the vote in the constituency corresponded to the view expressed.

Personal Views Toward Metro

The adoption of the Charter would have meant loss of office for all the local legislators as the plan envisaged the substitution of an entirely new pattern of political apportionment. Furthermore, rural legislators are generally of conservative outlook and may be expected to oppose radical changes in governmental structure. It was, therefore, surprising that the professed views of the councilmen and magistrates toward the proposal were almost equally divided. Forty-six per cent of them claimed to be in favor and 42 per cent said they were opposed. The rest were undecided. This was considerably more support for Metro

26

than the councilmen and magistrates themselves seemed to think existed. A summary of their personal views is presented in Table 3.

Three factors appear to be closely related to respondents' views on Metro — level of formal education, income level, and place of residence. The data show that those opposed were predominantly from the lower educational level, while those in favor were primarily from the higher

TABLE 3

Personal View of Councilmen and Magistrates Toward Metro

	Councilmen (N=18)	Magistrates (N=45)	Total	Per Cent
Highly in favor	7	14	21	33
Mildly in favor	—	8	8	13
Undecided	4	4	8	13
Mildly opposed	4	4	8	13
Highly opposed	3	15	18	29

Source: Interview data.

educational level. Of the 34 respondents who had completed a high school education or less, only 12 (35 per cent) were personally in favor of Metro. On the other hand, of the 27 respondents who had gone beyond high school in their education, 17 (63 per cent) were personally in favor of the plan.

Income and education were found to be interdependent variables, with ten of the 11 lowest income respondents falling in the lower education bracket, and 16 of the 22 highest income respondents falling in the higher education bracket. The data accordingly revealed that those in the lowest income group were more than two to one opposed to Metro, and that those in the middle income group ($5,000 to $9,999) were almost equally divided for and against.

Place of residence was related to the personal viewpoint of the county magistrates. Seventeen out of 29 (59 per cent) magistrates living outside Nashville were opposed, while 11 out of 16

27

(69 per cent) of the magistrates living inside the city favored Metro. Three of those residing inside and one residing outside of Nashville were undecided.

Degree of Personal Interest

Additionally, the interview sought to establish the extent to which city and county legislators were interested in the Metro proposal. The respondents were asked to select the subject of greatest interest to them from four subjects differentiated by level of government — the one-government referendum; the governor's race; the county judge's race; and the problem of outer space. Twenty-seven out of 63 (43 per cent) rated the one-government proposal of greatest interest in this list. In making their choice of four local issues, however, only 15 out of 63 (24 per cent) rated the one-government referendum first in interest as is shown in Table 4.

TABLE 4

Selection of Greatest Interest in Four Local Issues

	Sewering the Metropolitan Area	Integration-Segregation Issues	One-Government Referendum	Constructing Municipal Auditorium	No Answer
Councilman (N=18)	5	8	5	—	—
Magistrates (N=45)	15	15	10	3	2
Total	20	23	15	3	2

Source: Interview data.

As might reasonably be expected in a Southern city faced with a growing Negro population, the integration-segregation issue was of greatest interest. More significant, however, is the fact that almost one-third of the respondents mentioned sewering the metropolitan area as the local issue that interested them most. It is probably a reflection of a general feeling that the *raison d'être*

28

of Metro was to provide better sewerage for the whole county. Some seemed to believe that these issues were identical. In fact, sewerage was only one of the many major issues involved in the adoption of the Metro plan.

The respondents' personal view on Metro strongly influenced the selection of the issue of greatest interest. Of the 29 respondents who were personally for Metro, 19 (66 per cent) mentioned the one-government referendum as the subject of greatest interest. On the other hand, of the 26 who were personally opposed to Metro, only seven (27 per cent) rated the one-government proposal of greatest interest. Similarly, in making their choice among the four local issues, only six out of 26 (23 per cent) rated Metro first, but 13 (50 per cent) rated the integration-segregation issue as the local issue of greatest interest. The only other significant relationship that emerges in the rating of the local issues is that those who were personally in favor of Metro rated the sewering of the metropolitan area in first place ten times, with the one-government referendum a close second, being rated first nine times.

A relationship seems to exist between income and the preference rating of the issues differentiated by level of government. Only three of the 11 respondents (27 per cent) in the low income bracket rated the one-government referendum as being of greatest interest. In the middle income bracket ($5,000 to $9,999) 13 out of 30 (43 per cent) rated it first; and in the top income bracket, 11 out of 22 (50 per cent) did so. The higher income respondents were more interested in Metro, as compared to other political issues, than those in the lower income groups.

The interdependence of income and education resulted in a similar relationship between the interest in Metro and the level of education. The more highly educated respondents had a greater interest in consolidation than those in the lower education groups. Of the 13 with the least schooling (eighth grade or less) 31 per cent rated

29

Metro as being of greatest interest. Of the 21 who had completed 12 grades only, 43 per cent rated Metro of greatest interest, while 56 per cent of the 27 who had gone beyond high school rated Metro of greatest interest.

Familiarity with the Charter

The questionnaire included some questions designed to measure the respondents' familiarity with the Charter. Only eight of the 63 (13 per cent) rated themselves as "very familiar," but 41 (65 per cent) rated themselves as "fairly familiar." Eleven said they were "not very familiar," and the remaining three said they were "not at all familiar." In fact, few definite conclusions can be drawn from these replies since the questionnaire did not include questions designed to test the actual knowledge of the Charter. As might be expected, most of the "very familiar" ratings came from those who had the higher income and education levels. Significant, too, is the fact that so few of the local government officials rated themselves as less than "fairly familiar," even though a considerable number of them were interviewed before the charter was filed, and it was, therefore, impossible for them to have read it. This may have stemmed from their reluctance to admit their ignorance on a subject closely related to their public office.

Prediction of Referendum Result

When asked to predict whether the proposal would be adopted or defeated at the polls, 81 per cent of the respondents predicted defeat. The personal viewpoint of the respondents appears to have influenced their prediction. None of those who were personally opposed to Metro predicted its adoption, and eight of the nine who predicted adoption were personally in favor of Metro; the other was undecided. The date of the interview seems to be related to the question of prediction,

30

as shown by the fact that six of the nine predictions of success came during the last six weeks, when optimism was at its height.

Reasons for Predictions of Result

The reasons given for the prediction of defeat are given in Table 5.

TABLE 5

Reasons Given for Predicting Defeat of Metro

Reason	Times Mentioned
People not well enough informed	12
Fear of higher taxes	10
Fear of too much power in one man or in one government	8
City-county or city-suburban distrust and jealousy	6
Lack of public interest	3
Officeholders will defeat it	2
Other reasons, or no reasons given	15

Source: Interview data.

The 15 respondents in the last category, "other reasons, or no reasons given," do not affect the validity of the rank order of reasons as much as it might seem because the figure includes several whose reason was simply "not enough votes." Fear of higher taxes and fear of too much power were reasons given mostly by those opposed to Metro, while lack of public information and interest was listed mostly by those in favor of Metro. Most of the nine predicting *adoption* of the Charter gave as their reason the belief that an effective selling job was "finally being done," implying that their viewpoint had changed.

Groups Thought to Benefit or Lose from Metro

When the councilmen and magistrates were asked to name specific groups they thought stood to benefit most (or lose most) from the adoption of the proposed metropolitan government, very

31

few of them were able to name more than one or two groups. The groups mentioned most frequently, and the type of benefit or loss, are presented in Table 6.

TABLE 6

Groups Thought by Councilmen and Magistrates to Gain Most, and Lose Most, from Metro

Groups	Times Mentioned
Groups Thought To Gain Most:	
"Whole community" (none would benefit more than others)	23
Suburban residents (would receive urban services)	19
Newspapers, radio and television (increased advertising and revenue)	16
City of Nashville residents (tax and debt relief)	8
Politicians and officeholders (increased political power, better salaries, or stronger civil service)	8
Business interests (better tax rate and greater opportunities)	5
Other groups	14
Groups Thought To Lose Most:	
Politicians and officeholders (loss of jobs or prestige)	16
Negroes and integrationists (loss of representation in city government)	11
Residents outside the city of Nashville (higher taxes without more services; would "inherit the city's problems")	9
"No group would lose"	9
City of Nashville residents (poorer services while paying for services to others)	5
Suburban business and industries (higher taxes)	4
Other groups	10

Source: Interview data.

This listing does not indicate any real consensus among the respondents about the groups likely to benefit or lose from the adoption of the Charter. Politicians and officeholders were named on both lists, but twice as many thought this group would lose as thought it would benefit.

As might be expected, the 23 who stated that the whole community would gain, and the nine who suggested that no groups would lose, were almost all in favor of Metro. Eleven respondents listed Negroes as a group likely to lose from Metro; nor was this surprising, for the Charter's adoption would have more than doubled the white population of Nashville, while adding only slightly to its Negro population. Some respondents apparently believed that unless something were done to change the political structure, the growing Negro population in the city would in time elect a majority of the city council, and even, perhaps, a Negro mayor. Some respondents, therefore, viewed Metro as an expedient by which this might be prevented.

Two groups which appeared on both lists were the city of Nashville residents and the suburban residents. Both groups were listed more often as likely to benefit than as likely to lose. Suburban residents were listed on the gaining side 19 times, as opposed to nine times on the losing side. Eleven of the 19 who stated that the suburbanites would gain resided inside the city of Nashville. It is ironic that the Metro proposal was defeated by the suburban residents, in spite of the fact that more than twice as many respondents listed suburban residents as a benefiting group as listed the city of Nashville residents.

Newspapers, radio and television stations were mentioned 16 times as a group likely to benefit from the adoption of the Charter. This seemed to reflect a belief that the new form of government would result in larger circulation which would in turn mean greater profits from national advertising. The active support of the plan by both newspapers, traditionally opposed to each other on political issues, was said by Metro's opponents to confirm the allegation about larger profits.

Rating of Individual Group Attitudes

Each respondent was asked to rate 25 different groups of voters in terms of how strongly they seemed to support or oppose metropolitan reform. With a few notable exceptions, the groups were considered to be opposed to city-county consolidation.

The councilmen and magistrates had no doubts about the position of the two daily papers, to which they gave the highest ratings in favor of Metro. Respondents next rated the Nashville Chamber of Commerce and banking and insurance groups as supporting Metro, indicating a general feeling that the community's business and financial leadership was in favor of the plan. Rated almost as high, however, was the Nashville Trades and Labor Council.

Farmers were considered to be the group most opposed to Metro, and the six to one vote against Metro in the rural precincts in the referendum confirmed this appraisal. From the outset, no one successfully convinced the farmers that they had much to gain from the adoption of the plan. Suburban city and utility district officials were thought to be strongly opposed, as were the Negro voters. These ratings reflected a legitimate belief that the Negro population feared that Metro would result in the dilution of Negro political strength. In the referendum, both of the districts which had Negro representatives on the city council voted against the plan by 51 and 58 per cent.

Eight of the ten other groups rated as opposing Metro were various groups of city and county employees or officeholders. We conclude that this indicated widespread belief that the mayor and the county judge had not fully mobilized the support of the city and county employees in support of Metro. Some respondents even questioned the extent to which the mayor and county judge were, in fact, supporting the reform movement, suggesting that it might be unenthusiastic "lip service".

The preceding analysis has shown that several variables are related to the views of the local legislators on metropolitan government and to their perceptions of the politics of the reform movement. The data revealed that the local legislators

34

had only a limited amount of formal educational training, and that most of them had rather low incomes. Both of these factors were found to be related to interest in and support for Metro. The result was similar for both factors, with those in the higher income and higher education levels being predominantly in favor of the plan, and those in the lower brackets being predominantly opposed to it. This held true for both city councilmen and county magistrates.

The residence factor was also an important variable. Those living within the city limits of the core city were predominantly in favor of Metro, and those living outside the city were predominantly opposed.

The factor of government affiliation — city council membership or county court membership — did not seem to be related to the personal view of those interviewed. However, councilmen were fairly consistent in rating groups as more opposed to Metro than did the magistrates. None of the councilmen predicted adoption; 20 per cent of the magistrates did so.

The personal view toward consolidation was found to be strongly related to the local legislators' interest in and perceptions of the campaign. In naming groups which they thought would benefit or lose most, those in favor of Metro seemed convinced that no group would benefit more than any other and that no group would lose in the long run, except perhaps the politicians and officeholders. In contrast, those opposed to Metro named politicians and officeholders as one of the principal groups to benefit from the proposed plan, second only to the newspapers and radio and television stations which they believed would receive increased advertising profits. Thus, both proponents and opponents sought to hold themselves aloof from the interests of the "politicians and officeholders," a strange tendency indeed for city and county legislators. Finally, a strong relationship emerged between those in favor of Metro and those who ranked the one-government referendum as the subject of greatest interest to them, although many adherents of the proposal equated this issue with that of sewering the metropolitan area.

In conclusion, it may be appropriate to summarize some of the questions raised rather than answered by the research reported on in this chapter. The data reveal that the local legislators had a poor and, sometimes, confused understanding of the full implications of consolidation, but that many saw their political futures threatened. Was this an important cause of Metro's defeat? Could this have been obviated by a conscious educational program undertaken through the legislative bodies? Might the probability of adoption have been increased by including several city and county politicians on the Charter Commission?

Could the support of the local government legislators have been won by other means? Could the Charter Commission have made greater efforts to minimize the alleged detrimental effects of consolidation upon the politicians? Since the potential opposition of the Negro minority was partly nullified by including two prominent Negro leaders on the Charter Commission, and by careful political redistricting of councilmanic districts, could *other* potentially antagonistic groups have been pacified by similar means without compromising the Metro idea?

FOOTNOTES TO CHAPTER TWO

[1] In 1958, Nashville's City Council had 22 members, who were elected for four-year terms from single member districts, with the exception of the presiding officer, the vice-mayor, elected at large. The Davidson County Quarterly Court consisted of 53 magistrates elected for six-year terms. Nineteen were elected at large from the city of Nashville; 30 were elected from two-member suburban or rural civil districts; and the remaining four were elected from the four incorporated suburban cities.

[2] At the time of this research, two vacancies existed on the county court and two councilmen were in the hospital. Forty-five of the remaining 51 magistrates, and 18 of the 20 available councilmen were interviewed between March 1 and June 17, 1958.

Chapter Three

METRO AND THE SUBURBANITE*

The preceding chapter establishes that the local government legislators interviewed prior to the referendum had only a limited interest in the plan to consolidate the city and county governments. Moreover, their levels of income and education were related to their attitudes and interest in the proposal. Though significant, such conclusions only throw limited light on the reasons for the defeat of the metropolitan government attempt since it was the public rather than the politicians who defeated it.

Table 2 in Chapter One reveals that the 1958 defeat was caused by an adverse vote in the county but that a close battle was fought in the suburbs, with some districts voting for consolidation and others voting against it. This chapter deals with those who defeated the proposal, the suburbanites. The struggle over adoption in the two small cities of Berry Hill and Belle Meade (see Map 1) was posited to be fairly typical of the battle which took place elsewhere in the suburbs, and these two cities were chosen as the loci for the analysis of the suburban voters. In comparable turnouts,[1] the smaller community, Berry Hill, voted against consolidation by 219 to 117; Belle Meade voted in favor, 603 to 317.

This chapter focuses upon these two suburban cities and reports the principal findings of a study undertaken in November, 1958, which was planned with the dual purpose of: (1) studying suburban attitudes toward metropolitan government, and (2) studying personal integration into the metropolitan community. The principal tool

---

* This chapter was written jointly with William Paul Alexander, Jr., of Marshall University. The authors wish to acknowledge the important contribution to the design and execution of this investigation made by J. Leiper Freeman and Jeanne Clare Ridley.

used in the study was an interview schedule which was administered to randomly drawn samples of the populations of both cities. (See the Methodological Note, Appendix I.)

A total of 185 residents were interviewed in the course of the study. In addition to the usual demographic questions, they were asked about (1) their Metro vote; (2) their reasons for supporting or opposing consolidation; (3) what they liked best about suburban living; (4) their perceptions of community leadership; and (5) to what formal groups they belonged.

In some ways, the two cities were similar. They were roughly equidistant from the center of Nashville, and both were accessible by good highways. Both were served by the Nashville bus lines. Both possessed a new, but small, town hall. In 1955, they were called "pseudo-municipalities"[2] since their activities scarcely exceeded zoning, street maintenance, garbage collection and a limited amount of law enforcement. In 1958, both were served by suburban water districts which bought water from the city of Nashville at wholesale prices and then retailed it to the consumers. In common with the rest of the county outside the core city, neither suburb had a sanitary sewerage system.

There were also some important differences between the two communities. Belle Meade was an older community, having been incorporated in 1938, while Berry Hill was incorporated in 1950. Inspection of the two suburbs revealed Belle Meade to be an upper and middle class residential city. The homes there were large and fashionable, and individually styled. At the heart of the city was the exclusive country club with its large golf course and tennis courts. The streets were wide and tree lined, and the size of the lots was protected by strict zoning regulations.

Berry Hill did not have the social connotation of Belle Meade. A substantial proportion of its population was of the working class. In contrast to Belle Meade, Berry Hill possessed narrow streets, modest and similar houses, and small lots. In 1958, this community was unpretentious as compared to the distinctive appearance of Belle Meade.

Some additional differences between the populations of the two cities emerged from an analysis of the interview data, and these are presented in Table 7.

TABLE 7

Comparative Demographic Data on the Two Community Samples

| | Per Cent | |
| | Belle Meade (N=95) | Berry Hill (N=90) |
Demographic Factor		
Age: 40 Years or older	70	44
Residence: Had lived at same address over 10 years	52	18
Education: Some college or college graduate	76	32
Income: Over $10,000 per annum	65	4
Occupation: Business or Professional	71	37
Sales or Clerical	24	24
Blue Collar	—	37

Source: Suburban Survey on Metro.

Table 7 reveals that in 1958, the population was younger and more mobile in Berry Hill than in Belle Meade. The people came from a generally lower economic and social stratum, and had a lower level of formal education.

The Rationality of Metro Opinions

One way of looking at attitudes on the Metro proposal is to regard them as the product of a rational process in which the individual sees an interest to be served either by the adoption or rejection of Metro. Some initial clues to the nature of those interests were found in the reasons offered by respondents for their own attitudes toward Metro, when asked why they favored or were opposed to the consolidation plan.[3]

39

The most frequently mentioned reason by those *in favor* of the plan was that it was a sensible, efficient, logical or economical type of government. An additional reason, mentioned almost as often, was the provision for better services. Nor was this surprising, for a study of the campaign clearly revealed this to have been an alleged advantage publicized by the newspapers. The reasons mentioned by the pro-Metro respondents are presented in Table 8.

TABLE 8

Distribution of Reasons for Being in Favor of Metro*

Reason	Per Cent of Pro-Metro Respondents Alleging That Reason (N=90)
Metro is sensible, economical, efficient and logical	41
Metro will provide better sewers	39
Metro will provide better services (all others besides sewers)	32
Metro will bring about a general community betterment	28
Metro will provide "better" government and politics, it will provide better officials, etc.	23
Metro will bring about a fairer sharing of tax burdens	13
Metro will provide better schools	10
Metro will bring about industrial and economic progress	9
Others reasons	9

* Classified on the basis of answers to the following unstructured question, "Now, can you tell me the reasons why you are in favor of a Metro plan for one government?"

Source: Suburban Survey of Metro.

The reason most frequently mentioned by those *opposed* to Metro indicated that they were satisfied with the status quo and with the services being provided in the suburbs. The fear that Metro would bring an increase in taxes or that the government would become more expensive was also frequently mentioned. Some were afraid of paying for services which they would not receive. The old city-suburban cleavage and jealousy crept into the issue of consolidation as it often has elsewhere; and the suspicion of the city, or of its politicians, was specified by a large group. The reasons most frequently cited by those opposed to the plan are presented in Table 9.

An over-all comparison of the two preceding tables reveals that those in favor of Metro were more specific in their reasons than those who were opposed. Such reasons as better sewers, better services, fairer sharing of tax burdens, better schools and industrial progress are tangible and specific benefits. The reasons mentioned by those opposed were more vague and nebulous.[4] To

TABLE 9

Distribution of Reasons for Being Opposed to Metro*

Reason	Per Cent of Anti-Metro Respondents Alleging That Reason (N = 63)
Satisfied with present form of government and services provided in the suburbs	43
Metro would bring an increase in taxes; it would be more expensive	41
Afraid of having to pay for unreceived services	29
Suspicious of city; don't like city politicians	27
Did not like the way the problem was handled	6
Other reasons	14

* Classified on the basis of answers to the following unstructured question, "Now, can you tell me the reasons why you are against a Metro plan for one government?"

Source: Suburban Survey on Metro.

state, as many anti-Metro respondents did, that they were satisfied with the present form of government was not really an indictment of the Metro plan at all. The fear that consolidation would bring higher taxes was a more valid objection since the extension of urban services was part of the plan. It is worth noting that an increase in taxes for both the city and county was inevitable, whether the plan was adopted or not, but that substantial over-all savings were expected to result from the elimination of governmental duplication. The third reason given in Table 9 is ironic in view of the specific safeguard included in the Charter that urban type services would be provided, at least within a year after the urban services tax became due in any locality.

Metro and Personal Values

An alternative explanation of pro- and anti-Metro attitudes is to regard the rational reasons given in support of such attitudes as spontaneous answers devised to justify an irrational point of view or to express in words some heart-felt value about the kind of life-style desired by that individual. Other studies[5] have shown that one of the principal reasons for the mass movement to the suburbs is the desire to escape from the conditions of city life in an attempt to seek values that cannot be found in the central city. It has been persuasively argued that the *raison d'être* of the suburbs is to provide and preserve those values; and one may, therefore, expect the master plans of economy and efficiency to be opposed by those who emphasize essentially suburban values. By the same token, one may expect such plans to be welcomed by those who hold urban as well as suburban values.

In order to subject this reasoning to empirical observation, and to investigate the relationships of pro- and anti-Metro attitudes to "suburban" and "urban" values, each of the 185 respondents was handed a list of values and was asked to choose "the three most important considerations" in selecting an area in which to live. The distribution of values is shown in Table 10.

There is a considerable similarity between the rank order distribution of the values of the pro- and anti-Metro groups. The rank order correlation between the two sets of percentages is .69. In spite of the over-all similarity, there are important differences between the values held as most important by the two groups of suburbanites, The criteria of good municipal services, for

TABLE 10

Distribution of Evaluative Criteria Selected as Important in Choosing
a Residential Area by Pro- and Anti-Metro Attitudes*

Criteria	Total Number of Times Mentioned	Per Cent of Pro-Metro (N=90)	Per Cent of Anti-Metro (N=63)
Desirable and healthy neighborhood in which to raise children	149	84	75
Better property values for the money	87	54	41
Closeness to big stores, to work and to professional services	85	41	54
Good municipal services, e.g. sewers, sidewalks, police and firemen	85	51	32
Less politics, less red tape and less corruption in public offices	61	29	38
Lower taxes	47	16	49
Opportunity for civic participation	13	10	6
Fashionable and stylish neighborhood	10	7	3

* Ascertained on the basis of the following questions: "When people select an area to live in, many considerations are important to them. Here is a list of some of those things." Having been shown the list of values appearing in the above table, each respondent was then asked: "Now, would you tell me the three most important considerations on this list so far as you are concerned about an area to live in?" Finally, the respondent was asked: "Now, looking down the list, would you tell me which of these things a person is more likely to find if he selects an area to live in which is *outside* the central city? How about those he is more likely to find if he lives *in* the city?"

Source: Suburban Survey on Metro.

example, was ranked third by the pro-Metro group, but sixth by the anti-Metro group. Low taxes, on the other hand, was ranked third by the anti-Metro group, but sixth by the pro-Metro group.

More significant is the fact that two advantages more frequently associated with big city life were rated often enough to rank in the top half of the cumulative list in Table 10. These were closeness to big stores, work and professional services; and good municipal services. In contrast to the six other criteria, we had precoded these two as essentially "urban" values. These data show that even though they may have enjoyed the attributes of suburban living more than those of the core city, Nashville's suburbanites wanted some of

43

the advantages of the big city, such as the convenience of being near department stores, work and professional services. They desired government services, provided at less cost than they would have to pay for them in the central city. It is possible to see something of a conflict in the very essence of suburban living, a conflict between the things and values that people want in the suburbs and the city-type services that they expect as part of the American way of life. The suburbanites interviewed were a case in point. Only 20 per cent of those interviewed perceived all of their three most important values as being more readily available outside the central city, while over 60 per cent specifically indicated that one or more of their most important values was more readily available inside the central city.

In relating urban and suburban values to pro- and anti-Metro attitudes, we posited that those with essentially *suburban* values would view Metro as a threat to their values and would, therefore, tend to oppose consolidation. Con-

TABLE 11

Voting and Attitudinal Patterns, For and Against Metro by "Urban" and "Suburban" Value Oriented Groups

	Per Cent			Per Cent		
	Voted for Metro	Voted Against Metro	Did Not Vote	For Metro Today	Against Metro Today	N.A. or D.K.
"Urban" Value Oriented Group* (N=99)	43[a]	15	42	57[b]	25	18
"Suburban" Value Oriented Group** (N=84)	28[a]	31	41	40[b]	44	16

[a] Chi-square=7.557, P less than .05.
[b] Chi-square=7.263, P less than .05.

* Respondents having one or two "urban" values, and perceiving them as more attainable inside the central city.
** Respondents having no "urban" value perceived as more readily available in the central city.

Source: Suburban Survey on Metro.

44

versely, we expected to find a greater degree of support for Metro among those whose three most important values included one or both of those which we had classified as *urban* values, and who thought them more readily available in the core city. The data, though not conclusive, support the hypothesis.

Socio-economic Status and Metro Attitudes

A well-established approach to political behavior is to relate voting and political attitudes to economic status. Two kinds of questions may be asked. First, who are the voters, and second, what are the factors which determine the direction of their vote and their attitudes toward a political question.

With respect to the first question, distinctive voting behavior has frequently been found to be associated with positions on a continuum of social stratification.[6] In the present investigation, the data revealed that those who voted in the referendum tended to be drawn from a high socio-economic level and to have completed a greater number of years of formal education. They were politically more active in other ways besides voting, and claimed to be more familiar with the Charter than those interviewed who had not voted in the referendum.

Of greater interest to the present investigation is the question of determining what variables were related to the direction of the vote in the referendum and also to pro- and anti-Metro attitudes.[7] Family income, the level of education, and urban or rural background were taken to be three social variables of likely relevance in determining attitudes toward Metro. The data below reveal that only two of these were significant factors in accounting for attitudes about Metro.

Like other metropolitan government plans, the 1958 Metro Charter was the work of a Charter Commission dominated by lawyers concerned with legal considerations, and advised by plan-

45

ners, professors and professional students of public administration. Analysis of the Charter reveals that the values of efficiency, economy, responsibility and accountability were emphasized in the document. Indeed, it would be justifiable to call the Charter an intellectual solution to abstract as well as concrete problems. It was a formidable and complex document, and we hypothesized that, to the extent that support would be gained by better understanding, it would be more likely to win the support of the better educated than the less well-educated voter. The data in Table 12 support the hypothesis and reveal that the level of education is related to pro- and anti-Metro attitudes. Those with a high school education or less divided one and one-half to one against Metro; those who had attended some college were more than two to one in favor.

TABLE 12

*Pro- and Anti-Metro Attitudes, by Level of Education**

	Both Communities	
	Per Cent High School (N=80)	Per Cent College (N=101)
Pro-Metro	30	64
Anti-Metro	46	29
D.K., N.A.	24	7

* High school designates those who had attended high school. College designates those who had completed at least one year of college.

Chi-square=23.17, P less than .001.

Source: Suburban Survey on Metro.

The consolidation of Nashville and Davidson County was expected to be accompanied by some new taxes, and while these may fall heavily upon the pocketbooks of the well-to-do, they tend to be most strongly opposed by lower income people. Economic status and education are generally interdependent variables; and we therefore ex-

46

pected low income respondents to tend to oppose, and high income respondents to support consolidation. The data in Table 13 show that the low income group divided approximately two to one against Metro; that the middle income group was approximately evenly divided, while the high income group divided by more than three to one in favor.

TABLE 13

Pro- and Anti-Metro Attitudes, by Level of Income*

	Per Cent Low Income (N=55)	Both Communities Per Cent Middle Income (N=51)	Per Cent High Income (N=66)
Pro-Metro	27	43	71
Anti-Metro	53	41	21
D.K., N.A.	20	16	8

* The levels on income were divided as follows: Low, up to $5,999 per annum; Middle, $6,000 to $9,999; and High, over $10,000 per annum.

Chi-square=23.90, P less than .001.

Source: Suburban Survey on Metro.

We also posited that differences in Metro attitudes would be related to the type of background of the respondents, whether urban or rural. We expected individuals with an urban background to show more support for Metro than those with a rural background, the reason for this expectation being that we thought rural individuals might be more likely to view the growing metropolis with distrust and suspicion. In fact, the type of background did not seem to be significantly associated with pro- and anti-Metro attitudes. While the urban group was slightly more pro-Metro than the rural group, and the rural group was more anti-Metro than the urban group, chance factors could account for the differences. The data are presented in Table 14.

47

TABLE 14

Pro- and Anti-Metro Attitudes, by Type of Background

| | Both Communities | |
	Rural (N=45)	Urban (N=140)
Pro-Metro	46	49
Anti-Metro	45	34
D.K., N.A.	9	17

Chi-square not significant.

Source: Suburban Survey on Metro.

The preceding analysis is based upon the data of both communities. When comparable analyses were made for the two communities separately, it was found that the relationship for each variable was considerably more pronounced in the case of Berry Hill, buttressing the notion that political attitudes defined by a socio-economic index are not homogeneous. For purposes of explanation, other indexes may be preferable. For example, party identification is a better indicator of probable voting behavior in a presidential election than any index of socio-economic status.[8] We were faced with the question of what intervening variable in a nonpartisan referendum might explain significantly the deviations in voting behavior within any particular social category. The final section of this chapter[9] singles out membership in a formal group that is exposed to campaign propaganda as such a variable.

Voting and Group Exposure to Propaganda

The utility of formal groups in nonparty elections has been noted before.[10] In his study of the factional organization of primary elections in one-party states, V. O. Key concludes that "in intrastate politics absence of the organizing influence of party probably compels a heavier reliance than in two-party states on the use of private associations and of persons of prestige in nonparty

48

groups as the unit cells of factions and as avenues to reach the voter."[11] While Key examines a problem of popular support in a nonparty election similar to the one at present under review, his findings pertain to the organizational level rather than the electorate.

In the present investigation, we posited that members of formal groups who were exposed to campaign propaganda in the Metro campaign tend to favor the side of the issue to which their group had been exposed at significantly greater rates than persons of the same social status, who had not been contacted in this manner whether the latter were members of formal groups or not.

"Exposed groups" included all those which presented Metro to their own memberships and which had programs presented by spokesmen of the campaign organization for Metro.[12] Groups falling within this category included the Chamber of Commerce; the League of Women Voters, the Junior Chamber of Commerce, a number of luncheon "service clubs" such as Rotary, the Jewish Community Center, several parent-teacher associations, and the Men's Club of one school.[13] Since no data were obtained about attendance in group meetings where Metro was presented, all members of these groups were considered to have been exposed to the Metro cause within the context of their groups, even though it is possible that some individual members were not actually exposed. It must be noted that the data about memberships in formal groups were obtained by households. Therefore, the creditable assumption also was made that the respondent who was not himself a member shared the outlook of the person who was the household member. "Propaganda" was defined in a neutral sense to include specifically the presentation of information and attitudes concerning Metro to the groups mentioned.

The validity of the final hypothesis of this chapter can be established by showing that the effects attributed to group exposure to propaganda were not simply consequences of demographic variables or social status. To test its validity, the two community samples were each divided into categories of group membership. Respondents who were members of one or more groups, none of which were exposed to propaganda concerning Metro, serve as a control for comparison with respondents who were members of at least one exposed group. Nonmembers comprise a third category. A rough control of social status is incorporated in this comparison by the place of residence since all indexes of social status are highly correlated. The data are presented in Table 15.

TABLE 15

Metro Vote of Exposed Group Members, Other Group Members, and Nonmembers

	Belle Meade			Berry Hill		
	Per Cent Voted for Metro	Per Cent Turnout	N	Per Cent Voted for Metro	Per Cent Turnout	N
Exposed Group	81[a]	86	(43)	32[b]	52	(25)
Other Group	30[a]	60	(37)	16[b]	66	(32)
Nonmembers	7	13	(15)	18	36	(33)

[a] Chi-square = 13.44, P less than .001.
[b] Chi-square = 3.74, P less than .05.

Source: Suburban Survey on Metro.

Table 15 reveals that respondents who were not members of any formal groups generally voted for Metro in smaller proportions than respondents who were group members in both communities. The critical difference in voting behavior emerged between exposed group members and members of other groups.

In the high status community of Belle Meade, the difference in voting behavior between persons who were members of groups exposed to pro-Metro propaganda and persons who were members of groups *not* exposed to propaganda are highly significant statistically. While nonexposed

50

group members divided their vote evenly for and against Metro, members of exposed groups voted for Metro at a rate of about 16 to one. This ratio would occur by chance less than one time in 1,000.

Voting behavior in Berry Hill was anticipated by the hypothesis, and the finding concerning direction was as predicted. Members of exposed groups voted for Metro by a little more than three to two, while a little less than one to three of other group members cast their ballots for Metro. This distribution of votes would occur by chance only once in 20 times. The evidence of the two samples indicates acceptance of the hypothesis.

By taking occupation in conjunction with residence, a more refined index of social status was achieved.[14] A division of each of the samples was made according to three general occupational categories. By subdividing each of these categories according to membership in an exposed group or not, the effect of group exposure to propaganda was compared with the effect of social status. We posited that if group exposure to propaganda were not a significant intervening variable, there should be no significant differences in voting direction between the two subcategories of each occupational-residential category (Table 16).

The Belle Meade data support the hypothesis. In the two broad occupational categories represented in the Belle Meade sample the rates of voting in the predicted direction of members of exposed groups exceeded considerably those of others of the same social status.

In the business and professional category of Belle Meade, the direction of vote of exposed group members was exceptionally homogeneous. They all voted for Metro while somewhat less than one-half of the others did. This relationship would occur less than once in a 1,000 times by chance. A less extreme but similar pattern was found in the sales and clerical category of

51

TABLE 16

*Metro Vote of Exposed Group Members and All Others
by Occupation*

Occupation and Category of Membership	Belle Meade			Berry Hill		
	Per Cent Voted For Metro	Per Cent Turnout	N	Per Cent Voted For Metro	Per Cent Turnout	N
Business and Professional						
Exposed Group	87[a]	87	(31)	57	71	(7)
All others	22[a]	50	(36)	23	54	(26)
Sales and Clerical						
Exposed group	67	83	(12)	—	43	(7)
All others	36	55	(11)	19	44	(16)
Blue Collar						
Exposed group	—	—	—	40	50	(10)
All others	—	—	—	9	52	(23)

[a] Chi-square = 16.13, P less than .001.

Source: Suburban Survey on Metro.

the same sample. The members of exposed groups voted four to one in favor of Metro compared with a vote of two to one by others in this status category. Blue collar occupations were not represented in the Belle Meade sample.

The Berry Hill data are less conclusive in support of the hypothesis than the Belle Meade data. In the sales and clerical category the finding in the two subcategories was contrary to what was expected. The latter finding may be atypical since the number of cases in the exposed group cell is small. The exposed group members of the business and professional and blue collar categories both voted considerably more pro-Metro than the others, as was anticipated, though the cells here, too, are small.

The conclusion that group exposure to propaganda is a significant intervening variable concerning the direction of vote seems warranted. The only status category in either sample with enough cases in both the exposed group and other subcategories to permit a test of statistical significance lent strong support to the hypothesis that group exposure was a more important determinant of voting direction than social status. Three out of the four other status categories in the two samples supported this finding suggesting that the fourth category was atypical.

How does the phenomenon of the high rate of pro-Metro voting by members of groups exposed to campaign propaganda help to explain the defeat of Metro in the suburbs? A comparison of the data in Table 15 concerning the frequency of formal group memberships and exposed group memberships in the two communities sheds light on the differences in voting that emerged in the referendum.

Formal group membership represents the possibility of being contacted by pro-Metro propaganda; exposed group membership, the *fait accompli*. In Belle Meade both frequencies were considerably higher than in Berry Hill. Thus, the existence of more formal group memberships in the suburban areas of higher status predetermined the fact that a campaign aimed at formal group members would be more successful there than where formal group memberships were less frequent.

But Berry Hill is far more typical of the rest of the suburban areas than is Belle Meade. Therefore, there were undoubtedly many more voters in the suburbs in 1958 who were not contacted through formal groups than who were.

Conclusion

The data presented in this chapter show that attitudes for or against consolidation were related to socio-economic status — the higher the level of income or education, the more probable a pro-Metro attitude. The differences in the socioeconomic levels of the two communities surveyed can be taken as a general explanation for the success of the Charter proposal in Belle Meade and other high status neighborhoods on the one

53

hand, and also for its defeat in Berry Hill and in most other suburbs. A more detailed examination of the data, however, revealed other quantitative and qualitative differences between the adherents of the opposing views.

Proponents tended to be more specific in citing advantages of the Charter than opponents were in describing its shortcomings. Satisfaction with existing community services and opposition to anticipated higher taxes were the main reasons cited by those against the Charter.

One of the striking results, regarding the personal values of suburbanites, was the extent to which all of them appreciated at least some urban advantage in their neighborhood. However, an important difference between supporters and opponents of Metro was discovered based on a classification of personal values as "urban" or "suburban." Suburbanites holding at least one "urban" value were much more likely to favor Metro than those holding essentially "suburban" values.

An important finding was an intervening variable between the socio-economic status and the direction of vote. It was found that suburbanites who were members of formal groups exposed to pro-Metro propaganda voted in favor of the Charter in significantly greater proportions than others of the same social status — even with formal group membership held constant. This finding helps to explain the favorable vote for Metro in the suburban areas of higher status, where formal group membership was more frequent, in contrast to the low status of the remaining suburbs surrounding the central city.

FOOTNOTES TO CHAPTER THREE

[1] In Berry Hill, 46.9 per cent of the registered voters went to the polls, while in Belle Meade 48.3 per cent voted in the referendum.

[2] Daniel R. Grant, "Urban and Suburban Nashville: A Case Study in Metropolitanism," *Journal of Politics*, XVII, No. 1 (February, 1955), 86.

[3] The number of respondents actually having *voted in favor* of the plan was small (47 in Belle Meade, 19 in Berry Hill). Where appropriate, the analysis is based upon *attitudes* classified on the basis of replies to the question:

"What is your opinion *today* on consolidating the governments of Nashville and Davidson County into one government? Would you say you favor or are against the idea?"

The question yielded 90 pro-Metro respondents and 63 anti-Metro respondents, and these are the N's in Tables 8, 9, and 10 in Chapter 3 and in Table 19 in Chapter 4.

[4] The differences in the precision of the answers of respondents for and against Metro may be explained in part by the contrasting campaigns of the forces for and against. The Citizen's Committee and the newspapers stressed informational aspects, while the opposition avoided details, dwelt in generalities, and aimed their appeal at citizens' fears.

[5] Robert C. Wood, *Suburbia: Its People and Their Politics* (Boston: Houghton Mifflin Co., 1959); also several studies included in William M. Dobriner, *op. cit.*; John R. Seeley, R. Alexander Simm and E. W. Loosley, *Crestwood Heights* (New York: Basic Books, Inc., 1956).

[6] For example, see Bernard R. Berelson, Paul F. Lazarsfeld, and William N. McPhee, *Voting* (Chicago: Chicago University Press, 1954), ch. 4.

[7] The defeat of 1958 has been analyzed by other investigators. Daniel J. Elazar's central thesis is that Metro was developed and promoted by persons having areawide identification, whom he terms "cosmopolitans," but that the adoption of the plan hinged upon its acceptance by "locals" who had a constricted involvement in the areawide community, and for whom the neighborhood is the all important community. The thesis appears to be quite tenable as an explanation for the 1958 defeat, but is more difficult to apply to the dramatic reversal that took place in 1962. See Daniel J. Elazar, *A Case Study of Failure in Attempted Metropolitan Integration: Nashville and Davidson County, Tennessee* (Chicago, 1961). Using a more scientific and sociopsychological approach, two sociologists report that the factors of "education, anomia, and political alienation were all found . . . to contribute additively to an unfavorable attitude [towards Metro] which if expressed at the polls was likely to be a negative vote." These results are believed to complement and parallel our own findings. See Edward L. McDill and Jeanne Clare Ridley, "Status, Anomia, Political Alienation, and Political Participation," *American Journal of Sociology*, LXVIII (September, 1962), 213.

55

[8] Angus Campbell, Philip Converse, Warren Miller and Donald Stokes, *The American Voter* (New York: John Wiley and Sons, 1960), 121, 142, 143.

[9] For a more complete discussion of this topic, see William Paul Alexander, Jr., *op. cit.,* 22-37.

[10] Philip K. Hastings, "The Non-Voter in 1952: A Study of Pittsfield, Massachusetts," *Journal of Psychology,* XXXVIII (October, 1954), 301-312; Berelson, Lazarsfeld, and McPhee, *op. cit.,* 51-53; and Herbert Maccoby, "The Differential Political Activity of Participants in a Voluntary Association," *American Sociological Review,* XXIII (October, 1958), 524-532.

[11] V. O. Key, Jr., *op. cit.,* 57.

[12] The anti-Metro forces did not attempt to contact any formal groups, as far as is known. Thus, the problem of competing directions of exposure and influence is not discussed.

[13] The exposure of the formal groups represented in the samples was ascertained in an interview with the Executive Director of the Citizen's Committee, from newspapers which reported the meetings, and, in some cases, by telephone interviews with an officer of the formal group.

[14] W. Lloyd Warner, Marchia Meeker, and Kenneth Eells, *Social Class in America* (Chicago: Science Research Associates, Inc., 1949), 168.

Chapter Four

METRO AND COMMUNITY LEADERSHIP

This chapter shifts the focus of the enquiry to a discussion of the role of the community leadership in the Metro campaign since an alternative explanation to the defeat of Metro can be found by doing so. It presents data which support the general proposition that important and controversial decisions involving the future of the community are unlikely to succeed unless their champions and protagonists mobilize the active and enthusiastic support of most of those constituting the local community power structure.

The data presented purport to show: (1) that a substantial majority of the persons identified as community leaders by the suburbanites interviewed were in favor of Metro; (2) that most of the community leaders did very little active campaigning either for or against Metro; and (3) that a smaller number of the community leaders were identified as "key leaders in the Metro campaign" but that these were equally divided for and against Metro. An analysis of the nominations of suburbanites uncovered a relationship between the pro- and anti-Metro attitudes of suburbanites and the attitudes of the persons they identified as "key leaders in the Metro campaign."

A Nonstructured Situation

When they go to the polls, American voters are mainly called upon to decide the political future of those seeking office, and seldom are they required to make important policy decisions. On the rare occasions when they can do so, their decisions are influenced by several factors. Political opinions on questions of policy are most directly influenced by the events that create political issues, by the communications media through which these are presented, by political leaders and by political parties.[1] There are other factors which help to determine the voting behavior of an individual on a particular issue. In the case of the 1958 Referendum, the factors of socio-economic class and exposure to pro-Metro propaganda through organizational memberships were found to be related to pro- and anti-Metro attitudes of the suburbanites interviewed.

In the case of the 1958 Referendum, some of the other traditional intervening variables which might normally be expected to govern voter behavior were missing, however. The communications media are believed to have had limited effect since, with unprecedented unanimity, both newspapers supported Metro.[2] While often on different sides of the political fence on other issues, the two most important political leaders, the mayor and the county judge, both endorsed the proposal. Nashville is not yet part of the "two-party South", and political parties are believed to have played no part at all in the issue. The leadership of both labor and management supported the Charter. Thus, many of the sources of voter guidance were inoperative in the referendum, producing what can be called a nonstructured situation in which it was hypothesized that community leaders would exert considerable influence over voter behavior.

The Identification of the Leaders

Ever since Floyd Hunter undertook his classic study of Atlanta,[3] students of the local community have weighed the respective merits of the several methods that have been devised to identify the power structure of a community. No method has yet achieved universal acceptance and the debate continues unabated.[4] The two leadership groups discussed in this chapter were identified by using the nominations of the suburbanites, who were asked several questions dealing with the community leadership. The Berry Hill and Belle

58

Meade respondents were first asked to nominate persons whom they considered to be "the most influential" in the local affairs of "Nashville and Davidson County".

The 185 interviews yielded a total of 49 nominations. Eighty per cent of these nominations centered around 29 persons, and these were arbitrarily designated as the "top influential" group for the purposes of this study. The method used to delineate this group has some obvious limitations, and it is *not* assumed that the "top influential" group here discussed comprised what is now commonly known as the community power structure of Nashville and its surrounding county. It *is* assumed that the group included most of those who would have been identified by a more elegant technique. With the possible exception of both newspaper editors, there were no obvious absentees from the group as is revealed below.

In order to establish the role of the "top influential" group in the Metro campaign and to measure the extent to which they had supported or opposed the consolidation attempt, 27 of the 29 persons identified were interviewed.[5] They were asked questions similar to those included in the suburban interview schedule and other questions designed to establish their individual role in the campaign and the intensity of their activity in support or opposition to the Metro attempt.

The "Top Influential" Group

Interviews with the "top influential" group established that 15 of the 29 lived in the city and that the group was varied in its composition. It contained 21 political leaders. These were an ex-governor of the state; the mayor of the core city; the county judge; and the mayors of Berry Hill and Belle Meade. In addition, it included the two best-known Negro leaders in the community. Both were respected lawyers and members of the city council, and one of them had been a prominent member of the Charter Commission. Additionally, the list included two other members of the city council and four other elected or appointed county officeholders.

Since most of the questions in the "suburbanite" interview schedule dealt with Metro, it was not surprising that the questions on community leadership produced the nominations of several persons connected with the consolidation attempt. It must be noted, too, that the Charter Commission was largely composed of high status persons who might have been nominated as community leaders in their own right, even had they not been members of the Charter Commission. Apart from the Negro city councilman identified above, the top leadership group also included the names of three other Charter Commission members, as well as the Executive Director and the Chairman of the Citizen's Committee for Consolidated Government.

The two leading members of the City-County Planning Commission were included as was one well-known old-time boss politician who, though no longer holding an elected or appointed office, was recognized as a major force in city politics. Thus, a total of 21 political leaders were included in the "top influential" group.

The eight other leaders were drawn from the community's financial, business and professional classes. The nonpolitical group contained the publishers of both newspapers, three prominent bankers, two prominent industrialists, and Nashville's most eminent criminal lawyer who also had a political connection, since he had been active in Democratic party affairs.

The domination of the top leadership group by formal officeholders was not considered atypical but quite compatible with the findings of an earlier study undertaken in "Community A" in 1954. In that study, it was found that:

People inactive in community public affairs tend to single out *formal leaders* (persons in public office and high prestige positions) as 'most important,' more than do people active in the community. The actives cite *informal leaders* relatively more frequently.[6]

The domination of the formal officeholders was, thus, to be expected. The inclusion of the two suburban mayors and of the Berry Hill magistrate was significant, buttressing the notion of the conflict in suburban living between those things found in the immediate suburbs and those things found in the larger community.

The Role of the "Top Influential" Group in the Campaign

Twenty of the "top influential" group of 29 persons claimed to have been in favor of Metro, and they are identified as the pro-Metro group. The nine who were opposed are classified as the anti-Metro group.

Almost all the members of both groups indicated that "they tried" to get Metro passed or defeated. Only two interviewees indicated a total lack of concern. But when the respondents were asked questions designed to establish the nature and intensity of their efforts, their replies did not fully substantiate their claims. Activity was measured in terms of membership in formal organizations either supporting or opposing consolidation, and also by the type of influence used. Data concerning the first of these factors are presented in Table 17. The data show that less than one-half of all the leaders were active in formal organizations connected with the Metro plan. Moreover, it shows that the opponents to Metro were almost completely inactive in terms of organizational activity.

The almost total lack of activity on the part of the anti-Metro respondents was an unexpected finding. Perhaps this lack of activity stemmed from the belief that it was not really necessary

TABLE 17

Formal Activity of "Top Influential" Group, For and Against Metro, 1958

	Pro-Metro Leaders (N=20)	Anti-Metro Leaders (N=9)
No Committee Membership	9	7
Charter Commission Member	4	0
Planning Commission Member	2	0
Citizen's Committee For Metro	4	0
Citizen's Committee Against Metro	0	1
N. A.	1	1

Source: Leadership interview data.

for the defenders of the status quo to be active since the public's ignorance and apathy were working in their favor. The lack of formal activity in the 1958 campaign, either in support or opposition, was similar to the situation revealed by a study conducted in St. Louis[7] when that community faced an analogous choice.

A further analysis was made of the type of influence used by the top leadership group. The data in Table 18 show that, irrespective of their own position, each group engaged in a very limited amount of campaign activity. However, more active campaigning was done by the pro-Metro group, and eight of the 20 pro-Metro leaders claimed to have campaigned actively.

TABLE 18

Types of Influence Used by "Top Influential" Group, For and Against Metro, 1958

	Pro-Metro Group (N=20)	Anti-Metro Group (N=9)
Actual Campaigning (Two speeches or more)	8	1
Press or Radio Endorsement Only	5	1
Casual Conversation With Friends, Associates	7	5
Did Not Use Influence	0	2

Source: Leadership interview data.

It is considered particularly significant that 18 of the 29 members of the top leadership group made no speeches at all. The majority of those who were pro-Metro adopted a position of being in favor of the plan but did nothing, or almost nothing, to get it passed, and this reflects an attitude which is quite typical of municipal politics in the United States. Those against apparently did likewise, leading to the conclusion that a substantial majority of the top leadership group gave lip service to governmental reorganization, but did not otherwise become highly involved in the Metro campaign.

This lack of personal commitment can be explained in several ways. Community leaders prefer to use their resources principally when the cause is nonpolitical, noncontroversial, sure to succeed and when doing so will serve to pyramid their influence. The lack of activity can also be explained by the fact that the community leaders were hard pressed for time. Many of them would not have achieved leadership status had they not previously committed themselves to other community projects. Several leaders in fact explained their lack of activity in such terms, saying that they were already involved in countless other community activities, which monopolized their time, money and energy. Many of the persons identified as leaders were well-established lawyers, and therefore members of a profession which by its very nature makes it difficult for its members to involve themselves in a controversial local decision. Some of them had in the past been retained to represent the interests of persons and organizations committed to the status quo, others perhaps hoped to do so in the future. This is also believed to explain the limited activity, either for or against, of the top leadership group.

The Role of Key Leaders

The interview schedule administered to the residents of Berry Hill and Belle Meade contained a question asking each respondent to identify

63

"key leaders in the Metro campaign." Eighty per cent of the nominations centered on eight of the "top influential" group, and these are accordingly designated as "key leaders" whose roles are discussed in greater detail below. Surprisingly, the group contained as many anti-Metro as pro-Metro leaders.

The County Judge: In 1958, the county judge had been re-elected to an eight-year term by a large majority. He championed the cause of Metro from its infancy and worked for the adoption of the constitutional amendment in 1953, and then with the planning commission through the long period of planning.[8] Over the years, he made countless statements for the press and speeches supporting consolidation. On the other hand, some political observers later questioned the extent to which he had committed his own political machine during the actual campaign. Some suggested that he had perhaps exhausted his political capital in his bid for re-election and that he had kept nothing in reserve for the Metro struggle. Others believed that his "lieutenants" had prevailed upon him to play down the consolidation issue since it would be foolish for him to work to destroy the office that he had so recently won. It is hard, of course, to weigh the merits of these observations. Some evidence which indicated that he did not fully commit his political machine was found in the fact that his own voting precinct did not carry for Metro.

The Mayor of Nashville: In contrast to his counterpart in the county, the chief executive of the city more than once expressed reservations about the Charter while it was being drafted. Before completing its work, the Charter Commission heeded his criticism and made some changes, thus allowing the mayor to give the proposed Charter his "wholehearted support." Politicians interviewed prior to the referendum occasionally questioned the extent to which the mayor was "really for" Metro.[9] But these were generally in-

64

terviewed before the mayor spent several days going around the city offices urging city employees to vote for the Charter. In 1958, it was generally assumed that the mayor would experience little difficulty in being elected "Metropolitan Mayor", and his support was therefore construed as stemming largely from his ambition for the new office. The strong adoption of the Charter in the mayor's own precinct and in the city as a whole is believed to indicate that the mayor committed his machine to the plan and that he personally worked hard to get it adopted.

The Lawyer: Another key leader was a well-known lawyer, and the President and General Counsel of the Nashville Transit Company. He served as Chairman of the Charter Commission which drew up the document. He supported the Charter by "personal contact" and by several speeches before civic clubs, PTA and church groups.

The City Councilman: One of the key leaders was a well-known Negro lawyer who was both a city councilman and a member of the Charter Commission. In spite of advancing years, he worked indefatigably to achieve the Charter's adoption. He campaigned mostly in the Negro sections of the city, and made about a dozen speeches urging the Negro voters to vote for the Charter. While it is difficult to measure the impact of his efforts, it is worth noting that in the referendum the two precincts dominated by Negro residents only narrowly voted against adoption. Some observers considered this a moral victory, for it had generally been assumed that the Negro voters of Nashville would strongly oppose consolidation.

The Banker: The main opponent of Metro was a wealthy gentleman farmer and the President of a local bank. His wealth was such that he personally could have financed the whole of the campaign against Metro had he chosen to do so.

65

He appeared on television, radio and also made his views known through the newspapers. His main opposition to Metro stemmed from his conviction that "as units of government are enlarged, expenses are increased and waste and corruption are increased." He also believed that the new government envisaged "too much concentration of power and removed proper checks and balances." He is believed to have been the most outspoken opponent to Metro.

The Berry Hill Magistrate: One of the most controversial members of the county court resided in Berry Hill and represented that suburban city in the county court. He opposed and campaigned against Metro from its inception alleging the plan to be communistic.

The Mayor of Berry Hill: The mayor of Berry Hill was an architect. He claimed to be opposed to the Metropolitan government attempt because it had "nothing advantageous to offer;" because of his opposition to "centralized government;" and because Metro would bring "many more appointed officers." When questioned about his activity he claimed to have limited his opposition to Metro to "conversing with friends."

The Mayor of Belle Meade: The mayor of Belle Meade was a car salesman of one of the biggest car agencies in Nashville. He served on a "committee opposed to Metro" but was not, otherwise, very active in attempting to defeat the Charter. He opposed Metro because all county and city employees "were not promised jobs under the new government" because "taxes would double with Metro." He also thought that Metro would be despotic and "damn near a tyranny."

The discussion of the role of the key leaders reveals that they were equally divided pro- and anti-Metro. Four of the eight were in favor of Metro and four were against. An interesting finding of the study was that in nominating leaders suburbanites tended to nominate those holding a similar point of view on the Metro issue. Analysis of the nominations of the "key leaders" reveals that in every case pro-Metro leaders were nominated as community leaders relatively more often by pro-Metro respondents than by anti-Metro respondents. Similarly, the reverse was generally true for the anti-Metro respondents. The only exception was the mayor of Belle Meade, and no explanation was found to account for this deviation from the general pattern.

Table 19 indicates that suburbanites nominated as key leaders persons holding a point of view similar to their own more often than those holding a different point of view. This is believed to indi-

TABLE 19

Pro- and Anti-Metro Leaders, Nominated by Pro- and Anti-Metro Suburbanites

| | Per Cent Pro-Metro Leaders | | | | Per Cent Anti-Metro Leaders | | | |
	County Judge	Nash-ville Mayor	The Lawyer	The City Council-man	The Banker	Berry Hill Magis-trate	Berry Hill Mayor	Belle Meade Mayor
Pro-Metro Group Nominating Leader (N=90)	69	81	19	8	16	6	2	25
Anti-Metro Group Nominating Leader (N=63)	45	75	10	5	23	18	10	15

cate, though it does not prove, that the leaders had some influence upon the attitudes of the public.

The general conclusion of this chapter is that in the nonstructured situation produced by the 1958 Referendum some of the traditional sources of voter guidance were absent. It is believed that this situation made it possible for community leaders to seize the initiative and to have a considerable impact on the voters. The data showed that over two-thirds of the persons identified by the suburbanites as the "top influential" group favored Metro but that only a small number of these had actively campaigned for consolidation. The group of "key leaders" was evenly divided for and against, and the impact of their leadership is believed to have affected voter behavior, although the data are not conclusive. In Berry Hill, for example, the opposition of both the local leaders partly serves to explain the decided rejection of Metro by the residents of that suburban city. A similar finding is reported by Elazar, who found important departures from "typical" voting patterns, which he attributed to the influence of community leaders who became active in the campaign.[10]

Most of the 20 pro-Metro leaders interviewed expressed both surprise and regret that consolidation had failed. While only one pro-Metro leader claimed to have provided a maximum personal effort in the campaign, many of the others stated that they would become more active in a subsequent attempt, should one take place.

It is possible that the influence of some of the political leaders may have been discounted since the American public is generally suspicious of politicians, especially when these stand to benefit from the changes they advocate. It was generally believed that either one or both of the leading political personages would assume office under the new Charter.

Speculation as to what might have been done to achieve public acceptance of the Charter in 1958 continues. A reasonable conclusion is that in the situation described nothing less than an elaborate campaign involving large numbers of influential persons contacting the electorate through numerous civic, religious and social organizations would have brought about public acceptance of a radical departure from the status quo. This conclusion is based not only on the findings of the present chapter but also on those of Chapter Three, which established the importance of propaganda disseminated through group meetings as an intervening variable affecting the attitudes of suburbanites.

FOOTNOTES TO CHAPTER FOUR

[1] Angus Campbell, Gerald A. Gurin, and W. E. Miller, *The Voter Decides* (Evanston, Ill.: Row, Peterson, 1954); B. R. Berelson, Paul F. Lazarsfeld, and H. Gaudet, *The People's Choice* (New York: 1948); Angus Campbell, *et al., The American Voter.*

[2] Another observer of the Nashville consolidation stated that when both newspapers united behind Metro, "a good deal of public suspicion was aroused . . . [which] made their coverage a handicap to the proposal. . . ." See Elazar, *op. cit.,* 37-40.

[3] Floyd Hunter, *Community Power Structure* (Chapel Hill: University of North Carolina Press, 1954).

[4] Much of the literature dealing with community power structure is summarized in Charles Press, *Main Street Politics: Policy Making at the Local Level* (East Lansing, Mich., 1962).

[5] Two members of the "top influential" group refused to be interviewed. One was the magistrate representing the city of Berry Hill on the county court; the other was a city councilman, who, however, had been interviewed prior to the referendum in connection with the research discussed in Chapter Two. Both men took public stands opposing Metro.

[6] Ralph H. Smuckler and George M. Belknap, *Leadership and Participation in Urban Political Affairs* (East Lansing, Mich., 1956), 8.

[7] Henry J. Schmandt, Paul G. Steinbicker, and George D. Wendel, "The Campaign for Metropolitan Government," *Metropolitan Reform in St. Louis: A Case Study* (New York: Holt, Rinehart and Winston, 1961), ch. 4.

[8] In his speech to the Nashville Rotary Club on June 21, 1955, Judge Beverly Briley discussed local government and urban problems, and explored the feasibility of metropolitan government for the city and surrounding county.

[9] See Chapter Two, page 34.

[10] Elazar, *op. cit.,* 11.

Chapter Five

DEFEAT, 1958 — SUCCESS, 1962

After the Metro defeat in June, 1958, the subject quickly disappeared from the pages of both newspapers. The attention of their readers was turned, instead, to the more newsworthy stories of the Democratic party gubernatorial primary which, every fourth summer, catches the imagination of the voters in Tennessee. The rejection of Metro left many problems unsolved and many questions unanswered; and the two governmental entities, which for a moment had seemed close to merging, were left to pursue their independent ways, seeking pragmatic, make-shift solutions to their growing dilemmas.

The Davidson County Quarterly Court raised taxes almost immediately, and during the next two years attempted to provide some sanitary sewers, bridges and arterial highways to the most densely populated parts of the county. It faced the problems of overcrowded schools and underpaid teachers, and the problems of providing more adequate services to county residents. The county judge and county court also struggled with the problems of bond issues to finance capital improvements. As in the past the county found it difficult to provide effectively for the needs and problems of the densely populated areas lying beyond the core city.

The city of Nashville also faced grave problems, many of them financial. In 1958-1959, it was estimated that close to 40 per cent of the city's total real properties were tax-exempt since they were owned and operated for governmental, charitable or religious purposes.[1] The city still faced the problems of an increasing Negro population in the face of a decreasing over-all population and of decreasing tax receipts from this lower-income segment of the population. The city still received no tangible monetary rewards in return for the many free services which it continued to provide to a large daytime population of suburbanites earning their living in the core city. Thirty years without appreciable annexation had left Nashville as a small island in the middle of a large, densely populated urbanizing area.

Though Metro was defeated, it was not forgotten; and not many weeks passed before the Nashville *Tennessean* renewed its crusade for consolidation. Less than a month after the referendum, an editorial praised the consolidation of the adjoining cities of Newport News and Warwick, Virginia, but reminded local readers that their own community faced "a continuation of inefficiency, few services, and waste."[2] The Nashville *Banner,* on the other hand, which had likewise supported Metro in 1958, now took the view that since the people had spoken and rejected the proffered solution, it was now time to seek solutions to the community's problems through other expedients.

During the two years following the Metro defeat, the city administration made several attempts to solve its own problems. However, in so doing, it gave dramatic proof that the city and county were unavoidably linked together and that the solutions adopted by the one were bound to affect the other. In some instances, the solutions adopted to solve city problems had a nefarious effect on some county residents, apparently leading to an embittered attitude toward the city. In time, this attitude led to a new outlook towards Metro in the county outside the core city, and paved the way for its adoption in 1962.

The first expedient used by the city was to increase property taxes. This was quickly followed by the adoption, in August 1959, of a $10 "green sticker" tax on automobiles, to be paid by all city residents and all other persons whose automobiles used city streets on more than 30 days per year. The tax was aimed principally at the county residents employed in the city, and its revenue was intended to help finance some of the free services that the city had long been providing

72

to county residents.[3] The tax was disliked for several reasons. First, it was claimed to be a violation of the "spirit of '76" since it imposed "taxation without representation." Secondly, it was criticized since, like other flat-rate taxes, it was most keenly felt by lower income people. Thirdly, the city police and the courts were criticized for enforcing the tax unevenly. Sometimes they adopted a very rigid policy, made arrests and levied fines; while at other times they ignored flagrant violations.[4]

In order to increase its tax base, the city sought solutions to its problem in annexations. On July 16, 1958, soon after the referendum, the city annexed seven square miles of industrial and commercial property (see Map 2) on the grounds that these areas "belonged" inside the city since they were already receiving city services. The number of residents in these areas was too small (4,587) for them to cause much of a reaction. Nevertheless, the annexations were immediately challenged and tied up in court, pending a ruling on their constitutionality. This annexation was upheld by the State Supreme Court on March 10, 1961.

In the early spring of 1960, it was rumoured that the city administration would annex some residential areas but that it would wait until the spring elections of March 31 were over. On April 1, two city councilmen introduced a resolution in city council with the purpose of annexing 42.46 densely populated square miles. Plans for an annexation program had long been on file at the City-County Planning Commission, since annexation had been the basic recommendation of a 1952 Community Services Commission Report entitled *A Future For Nashville*. However, the areas that were now being proposed for annexation were only partially based on the recommendations of the professional studies. In other instances, the lines were drawn for political reasons. At least one boundary line was hastily changed at the very last minute, as a courtesy to

73

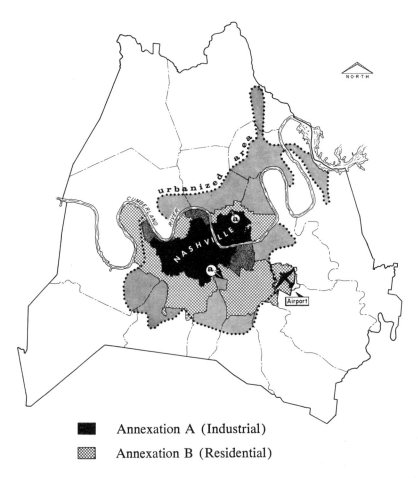

Annexation A (Industrial)

Annexation B (Residential)

MAP 2.—Former City Limits of Nashville and Annexations of 1958 and 1960.

the county judge, who otherwise would have become a city resident as a result of the annexation.

Acting quickly, the city council gave the annexation measure its required three readings, and then submitted the bill to the mayor for his approval. Amidst storms of protest, and in a precipitous manner, the city had added 82,512 persons and had more than doubled the city's area. In keeping with his previously announced policy that he did not favor residential annexations without giving a vote to the people concerned, the mayor vetoed the measure.[5] But the veto was of no avail since at its next meeting on April 29, the city council mustered a sufficiently large majority to override the mayor's veto. This annexation was also challenged in the courts, but was upheld by the State Supreme Court on March 10, 1961.

Observers of the political scene in Nashville generally believe that the mayor gave the members of the city council informal permission to override his veto.[6] The veto protected the mayor from the accusation that he had gone back on his word. However, by overriding that veto, the council was helping the mayor to satisfy his own avowed "consuming passion to see our city as the best in the world." The strategem may have convinced some people, but it did not convince the *Tennessean,* which editorialized: "The mayor sanctimoniously vetoed the bill. . . . Then he immediately put the screws on three reluctant councilmen so that *his* council would override *his* veto."[7]

In the annexations, the newspaper found an issue by which it could badger and lampoon the mayor. It mounted a steady attack of editorials, news stories, and cartoons which continued, uninterrupted, until the adoption of the Charter in June, 1962. The *Tennessean* claimed that the mayor had masterminded the annexations and had planned to have his "self-righteous" veto overriden. The paper attacked the manner of the annexations and the policy itself, which it alleged to be unrealistic inasmuch as the city could not possibly provide city-type services to the populations of the annexed areas within a reasonable time.

In time, the annexed areas did add to the city's tax revenue but not nearly enough to offset the tremendous cost of providing services to those areas. On May 3, 1960, the mayor announced that the revenue from the annexed areas would provide only ten per cent of the cost of providing new services, and the *Tennessean* took delight in

75

pointing out to its readers that the balance of 90 per cent would have to be paid by the residents of the "old" city.[8] The mayor's estimate was not surprising, for the city was suddenly faced with the prospect of having to grade, level, widen, pave and maintain close to 400 miles of "city streets," many of which hitherto had been winding narrow county roads lying to the southeast and north of the city.

The annexation of residential areas also raised new problems with respect to schools. Approximately 4,000 of the 14,000 pupils attending the 22 schools in the annexed areas had previously travelled to school by bus. The city found this service difficult to provide since it had traditionally operated no school buses.[9] Existing school debt, teacher pensions, and the zoning of school districts were complicated by the annexations. The legal requirements for county-wide bond issues required the bonds to be divided by the ratio of Average Daily Attendance in the two school systems. After the annexations, the area of rapid growth in school population remained outside the city of Nashville. Unless the city would agree to a distribution other than that provided in the General Law, the county would have to issue a total of seven million dollars of bonds for the whole county, in order to make three million dollars available for the county schools outside Nashville.[10]

The annexations of densely populated areas meant that the county was faced with an urgent problem relating to taxes. As a result of the annexations, the county was estimated to have lost 47 per cent of its district road tax revenue. On the other hand, it still had 72 per cent of the road mileage to maintain.[11] Thus, the county judge was forced to announce that he would seek another increase in property taxes for county residents.

While the mayor and the city administration struggled with the unenviable task of extending basic services to large areas that, hitherto, had

76

largely existed without them, the *Tennessean* continued to point out the shortcomings of the policy.

Over an extended period of time, the newspaper published several stories indicating that the residents of the annexed areas were very dissatisfied. Some residents stated that their services were not noticeably better. One was quoted as saying "All we are getting is garbage collection, and that's not as good as we were getting." Other residents were dissatisfied due to the increased monthly mortgage payments, caused by higher taxes, for which they were now responsible. The newspaper alleged that the annexations had forced many people to move, including widows and children, and that the annexed areas were now liberally sprinkled with "For Sale" signs of people who wanted to move out of the areas. Some realtors were quoted as saying that the saturated state of the real estate market in the annexed areas had forced down the price of many properties.[12] The stories, no doubt, were accurate, though the *Tennessean* tended to dramatize them in its determination to paint a picture of disenchantment with the city administration's policy of annexation.

While the *Tennessean* constantly reiterated this theme, it often came back to a related theme which inferred that the solution to all of these problems was to be found in a new Metro attempt.[13] The opinion was not universally shared. To the mayor, to a majority of the city council and to the *Banner,* the solution to the community's problems lay in following the policy that had been embarked upon. Just as often as the morning paper championed the cause of Metro, the evening paper reminded its readers that Metro had been tried, that it had failed, that other expedients were firmly under way, and that the community must now give the new policies a chance to succeed.[14]

The cause of Metro received support from unexpected quarters. As core city services were gradually extended to the annexed areas, some of the private police and fire companies who had actively opposed consolidation in 1958, suddenly found themselves deprived of private contract revenue. This deprivation was caused as the newly annexed areas began receiving police and fire protection from Nashville. One or two such companies were driven out of business; others began to champion the cause of Metro since they now believed that they would be incorporated into an over-all fire protection system.[15]

The Coming of Metro, 1959-1962

There can be no doubt, to anyone who experienced the events, that the "green sticker" tax and the annexations were very unpopular, and the *Tennessean* claimed that some suburbanites were convinced that they had made a mistake in opposing the 1958 consolidation attempt. The *Tennessean* now was determined to bring the issue to another vote, even though many obstacles had to be surmounted to do so.

The first formal indication that a new drive was under way came in October, 1959, when Magistrate Glenn Bainbridge (acting, it was later learned, at the suggestion of the *Tennessean*) announced that he would circulate a petition among magistrates to authorize another vote on Metro. On January 7, 1960, the *Tennessean* published a letter by Bainbridge in which he discussed the potential advantages of consolidation. Later that month, he introduced a resolution in county court to authorize another vote on Metro, and to allow the county judge to appoint a new charter commission. The motion passed by 29 votes to 24. In the meeting, its main opponents were the magistrate from Berry Hill and the mayor's former law partner who was granted the floor by privilege.[16]

The favorable action in the county court was followed by the introduction, on February 2, 1960, of a similar motion in the Nashville City Council. Before being voted on, the resolution was attacked by two councilmen as being com-

78

munistic. It was eventually defeated by a vote of ten to nine on the grounds that there was no indication of a change of sentiment among the county voters. In fact, that indication was soon to come. In the county-wide elections of March 31, Magistrate Glenn Bainbridge, Metro's leading champion, led all of the 34 candidates for Magistrate from Nashville. Other champions of consolidation also received a large number of votes. In the races outside the core city, Metro's main opponent, the magistrate from the small city of Berry Hill, was defeated by a huge majority. Five other county court members who had opposed Metro were also defeated.[17]

This election marked the turn of the tide in Mayor West's popularity. In the race for county sheriff, the mayor-endorsed incumbent was swamped by a political newcomer who had indicated his support for Metro. In other races, only eight out of 18 candidates backed by the mayor's machine were elected to the county court from the city of Nashville. The *Tennessean* summed up the election as follows: "The mayor's political machine . . . gasped and conked out under the onslaught of independent votes."[18] This election was quickly followed by the residential annexations discussed above.

On May 3, 1960, it was announced in a city council meeting that another resolution was being filed to authorize a county referendum on metropolitan government, and that it would be called up on the 17th. The *Tennessean* gave prominent space to the story and reported that some sections of the county's thickly populated areas were now shifting to Metro in the face of the city's annexation plan.[19] A few days later, Glenn Bainbridge suggested that if the city council failed to act favorably in the resolution, the only resort would be "to send a legislative delegation to the state capitol next January and February that will provide some means for the people to vote."[20] The threat was to no avail, and when the resolution was called up in the city

79

council on May 17, 1960, the vote against another referendum was 15 to six. The *Tennessean* reported that the council had defeated the resolution for four main reasons: (1) Metro was being pushed in order to set aside the program of annexations; (2) the county had had its chance to vote on the plan in 1958, but had rejected it; (3) taxes in other Metro areas, such as Miami, Florida, had risen sharply, and (4) the council should await action by the newly elected County Court after September 1.[21] Since the city council had failed to act, the only alternative left to Metro's champions was to seek to by-pass the city council through the state legislature, as Bainbridge had suggested. In the months preceding the August, 1960 primary, the question of Metro was made a campaign issue, with the result that almost all the members of the Davidson County Delegation elected to the state legislature had pledged themselves "to secure for the people another chance to vote on consolidation." When the state legislature met in January, 1961, nearly all of the delegation worked to make good their promise.

It required an amendment to the General Act, plus the passage of a private act, to set the wheels in motion again. The General Act amendment made it possible for a charter commission to be created by private act of the Tennessee General Assembly rather than by the action of the local governments of the city and county. The Private Act for Davidson County created the Charter Commission, subject to approval by vote of the people. To the *Banner,* this legislative action was "to provide a means of by-passing the Nashville City-Council," and therefore an "arrogant trespass."[22]

On March 16, 1961, the *Tennessean* triumphantly announced that a new vote on Metro now seemed certain. In fact, there were still several hurdles to be overcome. The Private Act creating the Charter Commission had to be submitted to the people for ratification. Though the recalci-

80

trant city council had been by-passed, an additional obstacle had now been introduced, in the form of a preliminary referendum. The referendum on August 17, 1961, was thus a dry run, for it was merely on the question of whether to ratify a legislative act that would activate a charter commission to prepare another charter.

The campaign preceding the August 17, 1961, referendum was significant because it saw the crystalization of new leadership and the formation of new citizens' organizations in the community which arranged a series of public meetings in various parts of the county to explain the significance of the advisory referendum. Efforts were made by some of Metro's opponents to confuse the issue, and a good deal of scare propaganda was distributed.[23] The *Tennessean* publicized the work of the extremists, reproduced some of the scare propaganda, and emphasized that much of it was from out of state, and was the work of "outsiders" attempting to interfere in local politics. The discredited name of John Kasper was also often linked with the scare propaganda by the newspaper.[24]

The vote on August 17th was light but decisive, and indicated that several large areas which had rejected the 1958 Charter were now in favor of another attempt. Both the city and the county voted to reactivate the Charter Commission by substantial majorities. Several of the newly annexed areas which had opposed Metro in 1958 now voted more than eight to one in favor of creating a new Charter Commission.[25]

The Charter Commission and the New Charter

The 1961 Charter Commission reactivated by the referendum on August 17th was identical to the old one except for two new members, one appointed by the mayor and the other by the county judge. One was the Director of Finance of the city of Nashville: and the other was the head of the citizen's group which had helped to revive and marshal the interest in Metro.

81

The new Charter Commission was rather slow in initiating work, partly because it could not immediately agree about procedure. It was late in October before the Quarterly County Court appropriated the necessary funds ($35,000) to allow the Charter Commission to engage professional and legal help, and early November before the group really began its work. The Charter Commission conducted several public hearings and held approximately 75 long meetings, as well as innumerable subcommittee meetings during the next six months. In view of all this labor, it is surprising that the Charter is very similar to the one rejected in 1958.

The differences are largely differences of degree, rather than of principle or structure. In many instances the 1958 Charter was edited and shortened. Commas were removed, and errata were eliminated. Two referendum provisions were dropped entirely and several administrative provisions were modified. But, basically, the structure of government outlined in the instrument is similar to the 1958 Charter. The Charter Commission members all seem to have believed the 1958 Charter to have been a good one,[26] and that its rejection was not a rejection of the Charter *per se,* but rather a vote in favor of the status quo.

The 1962 Charter provides for the consolidation of the governments of Nashville and Davidson County into a "Metropolitan Government of Nashville and Davidson County." Provision is made for an expandable *urban services district* which will coincide initially with the boundaries of the city, where residents will receive and pay for essentially urban-type services. The *general services district* will cover the whole county, where residents will receive and pay for designated area-wide services.

The urban services district will provide additional police and fire protection, sewerage, street lighting and cleaning, and liquor control. The area-wide functions include general administration, police, courts, jails, tax assessment, health, welfare, hospitals, schools, parks, recreation, public housing, transit, garbage collection, libraries, etc.

The most significant difference that emerges in comparing the 1958 and 1962 Charters is the enlargement of the legislative body which will be composed of 40 members, 35 to be chosen from councilmanic districts, and five to be elected at large. A vice mayor will also be elected at large, to serve as presiding officer. All of these bring the total membership of the council to 41.

Executive authority will be vested in a metropolitan county mayor elected by the voters for a four-year term but limited to three successive terms in office. The mayor will have the usual powers of a strong mayor. He will appoint departmental directors, as well as most of the members of boards and commissions. These board and commission appointments are subject to council confirmation, in several instances by a two-thirds majority.

The most contentious issue faced by the Charter Commission was on the subject of schools since the annexations had served to focus attention on that subject. A lot of time was spent discussing the respective merits of an elected versus an appointive school board. In the end, the Charter Commission voted for an appointive one, but not before a great deal of time had been expended on the subject of how to get a "good" school board. The Charter Commission added a provision unusual in Tennessee which would allow two-thirds of the school board to obtain a public referendum on the school budget if it is cut by the council.

The Campaign For and Against, 1962

The filing of the Charter on April 6, 1962, marked the end of the preliminary sparring. The struggle for Metro — which had been a reasonably polite and friendly contest in 1958, but a more warmly contested issue in August, 1961 —

83

now became an all-out political war with the infighting sometimes assuming vicious proportions. The proponents, led by the crusading *Tennessean,* but buttressed by an army of volunteers, fought in earnest, well aware that this was a last chance to effect the changes they had sought so long. The opponents, led by the mayor, encouraged by the *Banner,* and supported by a coterie of political faithfuls, fought back fiercely, no doubt aware that their political futures hung on the issue.

Some of the factors which explain the adoption of Metro in 1962 emerge from a comparison of the two campaigns. The analysis that follows is admittedly impressionistic since it is based mainly on newspaper sources, personal interviews and observation, rather than on survey data.

For most of the 1958 campaign, there was a curious lack of concern which apparently stemmed from overconfidence. Metro's proponents coasted along, without having to subject their views to the test of clever, documented and articulate criticism. Metro's desirability was generally accepted as self-evident, and no one really troubled to prove this. When, in the last week before the vote, the opposition unleashed its misleading propaganda, it was too late for the proponents to answer the allegations. In 1962, on the other hand, Metro was attacked and criticized from the moment that it seemed likely to come up for another vote. The *Banner,* the mayor and several members of the city council attacked the Metro idea during its preliminary stages, and the Charter itself as soon as it was completed. The Charter was alleged to be authoritarian, communistic, illegal, unconstitutional and "another nail driven into the coffin of states' rights." These attacks were answered one by one, with facts and figures, the findings of independent studies and with legal opinions. Long before polling day, every argument, both for and against, had been used and repeated. This foreclosed the possibility of a last minute scare such as had been used in 1958. In summary, the 1962 campaign was hotly contested but articulate. It dealt in specifics when discussing the existing two governments, as well as when evaluating the governmental framework proposed in the Charter.

In 1958, the main failure of the pro-Metro forces was a "failure to communicate with over half of the population,"[27] or, as the *Tennessean* stated, "the lack of a block by block organization."[28] In 1962, the campaign was organized much more broadly and in greater depth. On both sides, it was as if the professionals and the politicians had taken over from amateurs and do-gooders. As early as the end of March, the cadres of a pro-Metro organization were set up in almost every city and county precinct. The organization was spearheaded by an enthusiastic Citizen's Committee for Better Government, by Chamber of Commerce interests and by a Citizen's Advisory Committee. This confederation of pro-Metro groups organized and coordinated over 250 well-publicized neighborhood meetings which were planned to reach all types of voters in all areas. In 1958, the efforts to reach the public through organizational meetings were much more limited, but they had an important effect on voter attitudes, as is shown in Chapter Three. The emphasis on localized and face-to-face campaigning is believed to have been crucial to the success of the second campaign.

The 1962 campaign also marked the complete emancipation of women in local politics. For the first time, the League of Women Voters, the Council of Jewish Women and other similar groups played a major role in a local issue. Over 1,500 women engaged in door to door canvassing. The Charter was endorsed by over 30 groups,[29] and volunteers from 14 civic organizations, representing a total membership of over 5,000 members, campaigned actively for the Charter.

The opposition was also highly organized. In 1962, it fought Metro out in the open. It fought the consolidation at the grass roots level, through the hierarchy of the city administration and the

85

mayor's political machine, and finally through the courts.[30]

The mayor called special secret meetings to discuss strategy, from which the press was barred. He arranged for the publication of literature damning the Charter and used the police and firemen of the city to distribute the leaflets. The anti-Metro literature was also distributed through the schools by some of the city teachers and by some Boy Scouts at a meeting addressed by a White House Aide, attended largely by Negroes. The Mayor personally worked hard to bring about the defeat of the Charter. He invited the wives of the city police to a banquet where he made a full-scale attack on Metro, with the use of impressive charts.

The city police also engaged in political activities, and occasionally harassed speakers at pro-Metro meetings. The city employees were asked to do their utmost to defeat the Charter. Thus, the anti-Metro forces, led by the mayor, but supported by his minions and by the *Banner,* waged a much more highly organized and much more open campaign than had been the case in 1958.[31]

Another basic difference between the 1958 and 1962 campaigns is that the latter was overtly political. Political parties played no part in either campaign, but in 1962, political organizations, groups and machines were used extensively. The mayor knew that he had to defeat the Charter or face political extinction, and every effort was made to achieve his goal. His opposition, realizing his dilemma, forced his hand by challenging him to make good his offer to debate the Charter on television. In the end, the mayor saw fit to back down, but not before the *Tennessean* had made the most of the situation.[32]

A final difference between the two campaigns, and an important one, is on the question of issues. In 1958, the situation lacked urgency. The question was nebulous and hinged on the desirability of adopting an abstract solution to real and anticipated problems. In 1962, the issues were crit-

86

ical and clear-cut, though they varied for different groups. For the voter in the old core city, the question was whether or not to keep Ben West as mayor. A vote for the Charter was a vote against the mayor.

For the voter in the newly annexed areas, the issue was whether to become a first-class citizen of a new metropolitan government, or to retain the second-class under-represented status inherent in annexation. Another issue was whether to retain as mayor a man who had broken his pledge (to give the people a vote on annexation) or whether to drive him from office, in order to choose new political leaders.

For the voter in the rest of the county, there were also two issues: whether he wanted to be liable to annexation at any time, yet receive no guarantee of better services; or whether he wanted to adopt Metro, which guaranteed services within one year after any property became a part of the urban services district. The second issue was a choice between taxation without representation (such as the "green sticker" tax provided) and between a new plan, wherein each voter would participate in the election of six members of the new council, as provided in the Charter.

These issues may not have been clear to all, but the *Tennessean* tried desperately to make them so. In a barrage of editorials, news stories, cartoons, special feature articles such as is rare in American journalism, the *Tennessean* pursued its goal zealously, obsessed by its intention to defeat the mayor and to achieve a Metro victory.[33]

The Outcome

The adoption of the Charter in 1962 was in marked contrast to the previous vote in 1958. In heavy voting, the Charter achieved the necessary double majorities prescribed by law. Interestingly enough, the voting returns were almost a reverse of 1958. In that election, the city voted in favor and the county against. In 1962, the old city voted narrowly against adoption, testifying to the strength of the mayor's organization. But this slightly negative vote was more than offset by the annexed areas, which were now counted as city votes. These areas amassed pluralities of six and seven to one in favor of consolidation yielding an over-all figure for the city of 21,064 in favor to 15,599 against.

In the county, the issue was in doubt until polling day since some of the strongest supporters for consolidation in 1958 lived in the areas annexed by the city. As a result of the annexation, their vote was counted with the insiders rather than with the outsiders. Nevertheless, the extensive educational program of various civic-oriented groups, the fear of annexation, of continued taxation without representation was enough to cause a pronounced reversal of the 1958 voting. In the county, outside the city of Nashville, the vote was 15,914 in favor of consolidation and 12,514 against.

Epilogue

Alexis de Toqueville, a perceptive commentator on the American scene, remarked that "scarcely any political question arises in the United States that is not resolved, sooner or later, into a judicial question."[34] The consolidation of Nashville and Davidson County was a case in point. Having run the gamut of a dress rehearsal in 1958, a reprise that involved the two local legislative bodies, the state legislature, an advisory vote by the electorate, the drafting of a new proposal, a bitter campaign, and the adoption of the Charter at the polls, the consolidation nevertheless had to undergo the acid test of judicial challenge, first in Chancery Court, and then in the Tennessee Supreme Court. Thus, those who had voted for consolidation on June 28 were forced to wait until October 5 to learn whether or not they had cast their vote in vain.

The unanimous decision of the Supreme Court upheld the finding of the lower court. The opinion ruled on and upheld the constitutionality of each step which led to consolidation, but hinged principally on the meaning of the 1953 Constitutional Amendment providing for the consolidation of cities and counties in Tennessee. This amendment was interpreted as giving wide latitude to the legislature in setting up the machinery of consolidation, allowing local problems to be taken into consideration. Thus, the provision of two service districts and two tax rates was quite reasonable and quite compatible with the intentions of the members of the Constitutional Convention.

The Court concluded its opinion by stating that it was impossible to overstress the fact that the Constitutional Amendment and every subsequent step which gave rise to consolidation had been approved by the people. Also, by voting favorably on these documents, the people had acted in good faith believing them to be constitutional. The opinion then added that "after all, this is the people's government. Their wishes, constitutionally expressed, must prevail, no matter how much it upsets the previous status quo."

The decision of the Court was of great importance to the parties in the case, and also of considerable interest to the residents and decision-makers of the two other metropolitan areas in Tennessee which are contemplating city-county consolidation. The Court's interpretation of the Constitutional Amendment is believed to provide a good deal of latitude to other local communities to tailor their consolidation plans to their own local needs and problems.

With the legal dispute settled, the way was cleared for consolidation. The first officials were immediately sworn into office, and transitional arrangements were quickly implemented. Those expecting to seek office in the November elections quickly swung their campaigns into high gear, and it seemed certain that the new govern-

89

ment would become effective April 1, 1963. Many in the community face the future with unlimited optimism.

A note of caution may be appropriate, for it would be very naive to believe that the adoption of metropolitan government will immediately provide solutions to the problems of the community. At best, the Charter will provide for a more efficient administrative structure, and for new crucibles in which the public policy can be forged out of conflicting viewpoints. At worst, it will be abandoned before being given a chance to succeed. A more reasonable expectation is that it will have to be supplemented by other expedients. Most other consolidations have not proven to be panaceas to the metropolitan problem; and in almost all areas where consolidation has been tried, adoption of supplementary devices has become necessary to meet emerging problems.[35]

The process of change is inevitably slow, and the problems of the community will certainly not be solved overnight, even under a new Charter. It is generally expected that both the county and city bureaucracies will provide the bulk of the Metropolitan employees. Since both are heavily burdened by the presence of those appointed during years of patronage, it will be several years before the economies inherent in consolidation are fully realized. The adoption of the Charter was a bitter political battle in the annals of local politics, and some of the scars will be slow to heal. It would be very surprising if, under these circumstances, the Charter were to enjoy the unanimous good will and support of those transferred to the new government.

It seems most unlikely that the new Charter will usher in a period free of "politics", a pious hope often expressed by do-gooders during the long campaign. The harsh struggle over the adoption of the Charter, and the sharp contest that immediately developed between the hordes of candidates seeking elected office under the new government, indicated that the local political hive was swarming, and that it would probably be many years before a quiescent political climate was restored to the community.

FOOTNOTES TO CHAPTER FIVE

[1] Estimate of Councilman Farriss, quoted in The *Tennessean*, February 3, 1960.

[2] "They To Us Are Much Akin, But . . . ," The *Tennessean*, July 4, 1958.

[3] Since its adoption, the tax has yielded an annual revenue of over one million dollars.

[4] See editorial "Green Stamp of Confusion," The *Tennessean*, February 3, 1960.

[5] The *Banner's* main headline of April 1, 1960, read, "West Against Residential Annexation Without Vote."

[6] The *Tennessean*, April 30, 1960, quoting Councilman Draper; Daniel R. Grant and Lee S. Greene, "Surveys, Dust, Action," *The National Civic Review*, L (October, 1961), 470.

[7] See editorial "Pattern of Duplicity From City Hall," The *Tennessean*, June 11, 1962; see also *Tennessean* editorial of June 19, 1962.

[8] "What about That 90 Cents?" The *Tennessean*, May 5, 1960.

[9] The *Tennessean*, May 1, 1960.

[10] *Ibid.*, June 20, 1962.

[11] As estimated by City-County Planning Commission, and quoted in The *Tennessean*, June 12, 1962.

[12] "People Annexed By City Dislike West Program," The *Tennessean*, June 17, 1962; "Annex Woe Forcing Widow to Flee City," The *Tennessean*, June 18, 1962; "Annexation Forces Exodus From City," The *Tennessean*, June 20, 1962.

[13] See, for example, "I-Unit Taxation Benefits Seen," The *Tennessean*, May 25, 1962; "2 Governments An 'Absurdity'," The *Tennessean*, May 30, 1962; "I-Unit Called Boon to Youth," The *Tennessean*, June 2, 1962.

[14] The mayor opposed a new Metro attempt because it was an "attempt to wreck our planned [sic] program of annexation," The *Banner*, January 11, 1961. On January 12, the same newspaper published an editorial under the title "Metro is Dead—Let It Stay Buried," and on February 13, called the new Metro attempt "patently political as a stopgap barrier to legal annexation."

[15] "Private Firemen Endorse I-Unit," The *Tennessean*, June 3, 1962.

[16] Resolution 1-60-2, passed January 18, 1960.

[17] The *Tennessean,* April 3, 1960.

[18] *Idem.*

[19] *Ibid.,* May 4, 1960.

[20] *Ibid.,* May 13, 1960.

[21] *Ibid.,* May 18, 1960. A more likely reason, though it was not often publicly discussed, was that the adoption of Metro "would cause a majority of councilmen now serving to lose pensions [of $300 a month] if it was adopted before 1963." The *Banner,* May 11, 1960, reporting an interview with Councilman Gillem.

[22] The *Banner,* February 10, 1961.

[23] The *Tennessean,* August 5, 6, 1961.

[24] *Ibid.,* August 8, 1961.

[25] In the city of Nashville, 11,096 voted in favor and 3,730 voted against. In the county outside the city, 7,324 voted in favor and 3,848 voted against the creation of the Charter Commission. For an analysis of the returns see The *Tennessean,* August 18, 1961.

[26] On September 12, 1961, the *Banner* reported that one of the Charter Commission members had said "I think the old charter is good . . . it just needs some good reworking." The article added that most other members of the Commission had agreed with him. The two charters are compared in David A. Booth, "New Wine in Old Bottles: Nashville's New Charter," *Municipal South,* IX (June, 1962), 26-30. A shorter account of the 1962 Charter appears in "The Tennessee Votes on Charters This Summer," *Metropolitan Area Problems,* V (May-June, 1962), 4; and in Daniel R. Grant, "Nashville Area to Vote on Charter," *National Civic Review,* LI (June, 1962), 326-328.

[27] Elazar, *op. cit.,* 101.

[28] The *Tennessean,* December 31, 1961.

[29] A partial list is included in Daniel R. Grant, "Merger Approved in Nashville Area," *National Civic Review,* LI (September, 1962), 449-450.

[30] The mayors of Nashville and Belle Meade and other citizens challenged the constitutionality of the Charter and the General Enabling Act. In the case of Lewis Frazer, *et al. vs.* Joe C. Carr, Secretary of State of Tennessee, *et al.,* an injunction to prevent the June 28 referendum on the Charter was denied. However, the case was continued, to be heard following the referendum on the various points submitted. This hearing was held on July 17, 1962. In his ruling, dated August 6, 1962, the Chancellor upheld the constitutionality of the Act and the Charter. The decision was appealed to the Tennessee Supreme Court, and the case was argued on September 7, 1962. In its ruling, handed down October

4, the Supreme Court upheld the finding in the lower court.

[31] The efforts of those opposed to Metro were publicized by the *Tennessean*. See the issues of May 25, 27, 30 and June 14 to 21, 1962, for example.

[32] The *Tennessean* wrote that "West obviously felt he had to kill this charter or face political extinction here." See "West Strives to Slay Charter," The *Tennessean,* June 3, 1962. On the matter of the TV Debate, see various news stories, May 24-30, 1962.

[33] On June 20, the mayor stated on TV that no one in Nashville's history had "been subjected to the abuse, slanders, insults and unsupported accusations to which [The *Tennessean*] has subjected me over a period of years." The accumulated record seems to corroborate the accusation.

[34] Alexis de Tocqueville, *Democracy in America* (New York: Vintage Books, 1945), I, 290.

[35] John C. Bollens (ed.), *The States and the Metropolitan Problem* (Chicago: Council of State Governments, 1956), 71.

Appendix I

METHODOLOGICAL NOTE

The Berry Hill and Belle Meade Survey on Metropolitan Government, identified as "Suburban Survey on Metro" in this monograph, was undertaken through the auspices of the Politics Study Center at Vanderbilt University. It was designed by Jeanne Clare Ridley, J. Leiper Freeman and David A. Booth. The interview schedule consisted of 35 questions, three of which were unstructured. The other questions either called for simple answers or posed choices from prepared lists. The survey was undertaken by students and faculty of the Political Science and Sociology Departments of Vanderbilt University, between November 1 and December 15, 1958, about five months after the referendum took place. This sequence of time probably imposes limitations on the precision of the data.

The survey samples were randomly chosen. All private dwelling units in both cities were numbered consecutively in a serpentine fashion on maps yielding 1,086 units in Belle Meade and 507 in Berry Hill. Sampling ratios of one in nine in Belle Meade and one in four in Berry Hill were fixed to yield an approximately equal number of responses as well as a manageable number of interviews. Random starting places were determined by using a table of random numbers. Every ninth dwelling unit in Belle Meade in one cyclical sequence and every fourth dwelling unit in Berry Hill were chosen for the samples.

Either the male head of the household, the female head of the household, or the spouse of the male head of the household, over 21 years of age, and who had resided in that area before January 1, 1958, was designated to be interviewed. The sex of the respondent was also specified randomly. If no qualified respondent of the sex specified resided in the dwelling unit selected, an otherwise qualified member of the other sex could be interviewed. This procedure resulted in female ratios of 57 per cent in Belle Meade and 61 per cent in Berry Hill.

In Belle Meade, 13 of the dwelling units selected were occupied by persons ineligible for the survey or were vacant, five prospective respondents refused to be interviewed, and five respondents selected were never interviewed. The 95 cases represent 90.5 per cent of the original sample of 118 dwelling units. In Berry Hill, 30 dwelling units were vacant or occupied by persons ineligible to be interviewed, four prospective respondents refused to be interviewed, and four respondents selected were never interviewed. The 90 cases represent 91.8 per cent of the original sample of 128 dwelling units. This type of sample satisfies the conditions of random sampling unless the units have been systematically arranged.[1]

Since the proportions voting pro-Metro of those who turned out to vote both in the populations and in the samples are known, it is possible to estimate very closely the reliability of the samples if a credible assumption is made. That assumption is that there is no significant difference between the samples of heads of households or their wives and samples which might have included other adults eligible to vote living in the households (dwelling units) sampled. In the referendum 66 per cent of the Belle Meade voters voted pro-Metro. In the Belle Meade sample, 77 per cent reported voting pro-Metro. The critical ratio is 2.45, the sample value exceeding the population value by almost two standard errors. In Berry Hill, 35 per cent of the voters voted pro-Metro. In the Berry Hill sample, 41 per cent reported voting pro-Metro. The critical ratio is

---

[1] Quinn McNemar, *Psychological Statistics* 2nd ed. (New York: John Wiley & Sons, Inc., 1955), 361-62. For a further discussion of the sampling method employed, see Leslie Kish, "Selection of the Sample," in Leon Festinger and Daniel Katz (eds.), *Research Methods in the Behavorial Sciences* (New York: The Dryden Press, 1953), especially 198-201.

1.41, the sample value falling within one standard error of the population value.[2] The rates of turnout of the samples are excessive in about the same proportions as the respective errors in voting direction.

Students also assisted in coding data not precoded. The data were then transcribed to punched cards and manipulated by means of an IBM 101 Statistical Machine.

---

[2] The standard errors of the proportions were calculated by the formula with a correction for a finite universe from McNemar, *op. cit.*, 54, 99-100.

Appendix II

SELECTED BIBLIOGRAPHY

No Bibliography on Metropolitan Problems and Research could be definitive. The following works are believed to be relevant to the study.

I. NASHVILLE AND ITS PROBLEMS

Alexander, William Paul, Jr. "The Effects of Group Exposure to Campaign Propaganda Upon Voting Behavior in a Nonpartisan Referendum." Unpublished Master of Arts Thesis, Vanderbilt University, 1961.

Booth, David A. "New Wine in Old Bottles: Nashville's New Charter," *Municipal South,* IX (June, 1962), 26-30.

Elazar, Daniel J. *A Case Study of Failure in Attempted Metropolitan Integration: Nashville and Davidson County, Tennessee.* University of Chicago: National Opinion Research and Social Science Division (August, 1961).

Grant, Daniel R. "Merger Approved for Nashville Area," *National Civic Review,* LI (September, 1962), 449-450.

Grant, Daniel R. "Nashville Area to Vote on Charter," *National Civic Review,* LI (June, 1962), 326-328.

Grant, Daniel R. "Nashville Metro Charter Proposed," *National Municipal Review,* XLVII (May, 1958), 235-236.

Grant, Daniel R. "Suburban Vote Downs Metro Charter," *National Municipal Review,* XLVII (September, 1958), 399-401.

Grant, Daniel R. "Urban and Suburban Nashville: A Case Study in Metropolitanism," *Journal of Politics,* XVII (February, 1955), 82-99.

Grant, Daniel R., and Greene, Lee S. "Surveys, Dust, Action," *National Civic Review,* L (October, 1961), 466-471.

Halberstam, David. "Good City Gone Ugly," *The Reporter,* XXII (March 31, 1960), 17-19.

McDill, Edward L., and Ridley, Jeanne Clare. "Status, Anomia, Political Alienation, and Political Participation," *American Journal of Sociology,* LXVIII (September, 1962), 205-213.

Stewart, Alva. "Nashville Works Toward 'Magnificant Future,'" *Municipal South,* IV (August, 1958), 7.

Citizens Committee for Metropolitan Government. *You and Metropolitan Government,* Nashville, Tennessee, 1958.

Metropolitan Government Charter Commission. *Proposed Metropolitan Government Charter For Nashville and Davidson County.* Nashville, Tennessee: Citizens Committee for Metropolitan Government, May, 1958.

Metropolitan Government Charter Commission. *Proposed Metropolitan Government Charter For Nashville and Davidson County.* Nashville, Tennessee: Citizens Committee for Metropolitan Government, April, 1962.

A Report of Community Services Commission for Davidson County and the City of Nashville. *A Future for Nashville.* Nashville, Tennessee, 1952.

II. TENNESSEE: GENERAL WORKS

Combs, William H., and Cole, William E. *Tennessee: A Political Study.* Knoxville: University of Tennessee Press, 1940.

Goodman, William. *Inherited Domain: Political Parties in Tennessee.* Knoxville: Bureau of Public Administration, University of Tennessee, 1954.

Green, Lee Seifert, and Avery, Robert Sterling. *Government in Tennessee.* Knoxville: University of Tennessee Press, 1962.

Halberstam, David. "The Air Conditioned Crusade Against Albert Gore," *The Reporter,* XIX (September 4, 1958), 24-26.

Halberstam, David. "The Silent Ones Speak Up in Tennessee," *The Reporter,* XXIII (September 1, 1960), 28-30.

Key, V. O., Jr. *Southern Politics in State and Nation.* "The Civil War and Mr. Crump," Ch. 4. New York: Alfred A. Knopf, Inc., 1949.

Nelson, Robert. "Tennessee's Evolution," *The Christian Science Monitor,* September 14, 1962.

Nixon, Clarence H. "Politics of the Hills," *Journal of Politics,* VIII (May, 1946), 123-133.

Patten, Cartter. *A Tennessee Chronicle,* Nashville, 1953.

Perry, Jennings. *Democracy Begins at Home: The Tennessee Fight on the Poll Tax.* Philadelphia: J. B. Lippincott Co., 1944.

Pouder, Margaret. "Tennessee Reorganizes Its State Government," *Tennessee Planner,* XVIII (January/March, 1959), 67-84.

Tennessee Blue Book: Reference Edition. Nashville: Office of the Secretary of State, Annual.

Tennessee Planning Legislation: 1935-1961. Nashville: Tennessee State Planning Commission, March, 1962.

III. THE METROPOLITAN PROBLEM

Adrian, Charles R. *Governing Urban America.* 2nd ed. New York: McGraw-Hill Book Co., 1961.

Berelson, Bernard R., Lazarsfeld, Paul F. and McPhee, William N. *Voting.* Chicago: University of Chicago Press, 1954.

Betters, Harry R. (ed.) *City Problems of 1960.* Washington: The United States Conference of Mayors, 1960.

Bollens, John C. (ed.) *Exploring the Metropolitan Community.* Berkeley: University of California Press, 1961.

Bromage, Arthur W. "Political Representation In Metropolitan Areas," *American Political Science Review,* LII (June, 1958), 406-418.

Campbell, Angus, Gurin, Gerald A., and Miller, Warren. *The Voter Decides.* Evanston, Illinois: Row, Peterson, 1954.

Dobriner, William M. (ed.) *The Suburban Community.* New York: G. P. Putnam's Sons, 1958.

Downs, Anthony. "Metropolitan Growth and Future Political Problems," *Land Economics,* XXXVII (November, 1961), 311-320.

Greer, Scott. "Individual Participation in Mass Society," in Roland Young (ed.) *Approaches to the Study of Politics.* Evanston, Illinois: Northwestern University Press, 1958.

Gulick, Luther H. *The Metropolitan Problem and American Ideas.* New York: Alfred A. Knopf, Inc., 1962.

Hirsch, Werner Z. "Planners Say 'Yes', Voters Say 'No,'" *Challenge,* X (January, 1962), 42-44.

Huckshorn, Robert J. and Young, Charles E. "Study of Voting Splits on City Councils in Los Angeles County," *The Western Political Quarterly,* XIII (June, 1960), 479-497.

Hunter, Floyd. *Community Power Structure.* Chapel Hill: University of North Carolina Press, 1954.

Merton, Robert K. "Patterns of Influence: A Study of Interpersonal Influence and of Communication Behavior in a Local Community," in Paul F. Lazarsfeld and Frank N. Stanton (eds.) *Communications Research,*

102

1948-1949. New York: Harper and Bros., 1949.

Ostrom, Vincent, *et al.* "The Organization of Government in Metropolitan Areas: A Theoretical Inquiry," *American Political Science Review,* LV (December, 1961), 831-842.

Peardon, Thomas P. (ed.) "The Urban Problems," *Political Science Quarterly,* XXVII (May, 1960), Supplement.

Rossi, Peter H. "Community Decision Making," *Administrative Science Quarterly,* I (March, 1957), 415-443.

Schmandt, Henry J., Steinbicker, Paul G., and Wendel, George D. *Metropolitan Reform in St. Louis: A Case Study.* New York: Holt, Rinehart and Winston, 1961.

Seeley, John R., Sim, Alexander R., and Loosley, Elizabeth W. *Crestwood Heights.* New York: Basic Books, Inc., 1956.

Sofen, Edward. "Problems of Metropolitan Leadership: The Miami Experience," *Midwest Journal of Political Science,* V (February, 1961), 18-38.

Ward, Henry. "Metro: What and Why," *Louisville,* X (September 20, 1959), 7-10.

Wood, Robert C. *Suburbia, Its People and Their Politics.* Boston: Houghton Mifflin, 1959.

Bollens, John C. (ed.) *The States and The Metropolitan Problem.* Chicago: Council of State Governments, 1956.

"The Future Metropolis," *Daedalus,* XC (Winter, 1961).

"Metropolitan Areas Face Severe Governmental Problems," *Congressional Quarterly Weekly Report,* XIX (August 25, 1961), 1484-1487.

"Objectives of Metropolitan Government," *National Civic Review,* IIL (January, 1959), 29-33.

103

INSTITUTE PUBLICATIONS

Adrian, Charles R., Peter H. Rossi, Robert A. Dahl, and Lloyd Rodwin. *Social Science and Community Action,* 1960 $2.00

Bettelheim, Bruno. *Child Guidance: A Community Responsibility,* 1962   .50

Booth, David A. *A Guide to Local Politics,* 1961   .50

Chapman, Samuel G., and Colonel T. Eric St. Johnston, C.B.E. *The Police Heritage in England and America: A Developmental Survey,* 1962   .50

Duke, Richard D. *Automatic Data Processing: Its Application to Urban Planning,* 1961   2.00

Edwards, Alfred L. *A Study of Local Government Debt in Michigan,* 1960   1.00

Form, William H., and Warren L. Sauer. *Community Influentials in A Middle-Sized City,* 1960   .50

Hotaling, Robert B. *Urban Renewal in Private Enterprise,* 1962   .50

Olmsted, Donald W. *Social Groups, Roles, and Leadership: An Introduction to the Concepts,* 1961   1.50

Press, Charles. *Main Street Politics: Policy Making at the Local Level,* 1962   2.00

Press, Charles. *When One-Third of a City Moves to the Suburbs: A Report on the Grand Rapids Metropolitan Area,* 1959   1.00

Smith, Joe. *Some Social Aspects of Mass Transit in Selected American Cities,* 1959   1.00

Strassmann, W. Paul. *Economic Growth in Northern Michigan: Trends in Tourism, Agriculture, Mining, and Manufacturing,* 1958   1.00

Strassmann, W. Paul. *The Urban Economies of Southern Michigan,* 1958   .50

Suggitt, Frank W., John L. Hazard, and Charles R. Adrian. *Land and Water Policies for the Future,* 1959   1.00

Taylor, Milton C. *Local Income Taxes as a Source of Revenue for Michigan Communities,* 1961 .50

VerBurg, Kenneth, *A Study of the Legal Powers of Michigan Local Government,* 1960 1.00

INSTITUTE REPRINTS

"Community Involvement in Community Development Programs," by Christopher Sower and Walter E. Freeman, *Rural Sociology,* Vol. XXIII, No. 1, March, 1958.

"Community Power and Strategies in Race Relations," by James B. McKee, *Social Problems,* Vol. VI, No. 3, 1959.

"Metropology: Folklore and Field Research," by Charles R. Adrian, *Public Administration Review,* Vol. XXI, No. 3, Summer, 1961.

"Organizational Leadership and Social Structure in a Small City," by Donald W. Olmsted, *American Sociological Review,* June, 1954.

"The Insulation of Local Politics Under the Nonpartisan Ballot," by Oliver P. Williams, Charles R. Adrian, *The American Political Science Review,* Vol. LIII, No. 4, December, 1959.

"Power Structure and Community Change: A Replication Study of Community A," by David A. Booth and Charles R. Adrian, *Midwest Journal of Political Science,* Vol. VI, No. 3, August, 1962.

"Whether to Use Police Dogs," by Samuel G. Chapman, *Police,* September-October, 1961.

"Leadership and Decision-Making in Manager Cities," by Charles R. Adrian, *Public Administration Review,* Vol. XVIII, No. 3, Summer, 1958.

"Urbanizing the Land-Grant Philosophy," by Charles R. Adrian and Margaret Y. Henderson, *Adult Leadership,* October, 1961.

"A Typology for Nonpartisan Elections," by Charles R. Adrian, *The Western Political Quarterly,* Vol. XII, No. 2, June, 1959.

"Research on The Metropolis Foundation for Conservation," by Charles Press, *Public Administration Review,* Vol. XXII, No. 2, Spring, 1962.

"Simplifying the Discovery of Elites," by David A. Booth and Charles R. Adrian, *The American Behavioral Scientist,* Vol. V, No. 2, October, 1961.

"Elections and Community Power," by David A. Booth and Charles R. Adrian, *The Journal of Politics,* Vol. XXV, No. 1, February, 1963.

THE INSTITUTE FOR COMMUNITY DEVELOPMENT AND SERVICES

Director: Charles R. Adrian
Associate Director: Uel Blank
Chief of Research: Walter E. Freeman

STAFF

Alchin, Edmond W., *Community Development Specialist*
Beck, John D., *Graphics Specialist*
Blome, Donald A., *Geographer*
Booth, David A., *Political Scientist*
Brackney, Burton B., *Community Development Specialist*
Chapman, Samuel G., *Police Administration Specialist*
Donoghue, John D., *Anthropologist*
Duke, Richard D., *Urban Planner*
Edwards, Alfred L., *Economist*
Goldschmidt, Carl, *Urban Planner*
Hill, C. Edward, *Librarian*
Hotaling, Robert B., *Urban Planner*
Howell, John C., *Sociologist*
Ishino, Iwao, *Anthropologist*
King, Gary W., *Sociologist*
Levak, Albert E., *Social Scientist*
Marquis, Stewart D., *Urban Planner*
McKee, James B., *Sociologist*
McMonagle, Carl, *Highway Engineer*
Press, Charles, *Political Scientist*
Snyder, Abram P., *Community Development Specialist (Marquette)*
Sokolow, Alvin D., *Political Scientist*
Thaden, John F., *Sociologist*

Editor: Isabelle Brymer